PENGUIN BOOKS

RENEGADE

Mark E. Smith was born in north Manchester in 1957. He has been the leader and lead vocalist of The Fall for thirty years. In 2001 he married Eleni Poulou. When not touring, they live in Manchester.

Austin Collings was born in north Manchester in 1980. He has written for the *Guardian*, *Frieze* and *Flux*, among other publications, and currently lives in Manchester.

Renegade

The Lives and Tales of Mark E. Smith

MARK E. SMITH
with Austin Collings

photographs by Tom Sheehan

PENGUIN BOOKS

PENGUIN BOOKS

Published by the Penguin Group
Penguin Books Ltd, 80 Strand, London WC2R 0RL, England
Penguin Group (USA) Inc., 375 Hudson Street, New York, New York 10014, USA
Penguin Group (Canada), 90 Eglinton Avenue East, Suite 700, Toronto, Ontario, Canada M4P 2Y3
(a division of Pearson Penguin Canada Inc.)
Penguin Ireland, 25 St Stephen's Green, Dublin 2, Ireland
(a division of Penguin Books Ltd)
Penguin Group (Australia), 250 Camberwell Road, Camberwell, Victoria 3124, Australia
(a division of Pearson Australia Group Pty Ltd)
Penguin Books India Pvt Ltd, 11 Community Centre, Panchsheel Park, New Delhi – 110 017, India
Penguin Group (NZ), 67 Apollo Drive, Rosedale, North Shore 0632, New Zealand
(a division of Pearson New Zealand Ltd)
Penguin Books (South Africa) (Pty) Ltd, 24 Sturdee Avenue, Rosebank, Johannesburg 2196, South Africa

Penguin Books Ltd, Registered Offices: 80 Strand, London WC2R 0RL, England

www.penguin.com

First published by Viking 2008
Published in Penguin Books 2009
2

Typeset by Rowland Phototypesetting Ltd, Bury St Edmunds, Suffolk
Printed in England by Clays Ltd, St Ives plc

ISBN: 978-0-141-02866-8

www.greenpenguin.co.uk

Penguin Books is committed to a sustainable future
for our business, our readers and our planet.
The book in your hands is made from paper
certified by the Forest Stewardship Council.

. . . both everything and nothing in a person's past and background may be significant.

B. S. Johnson, *Christie Malry's Own Double Entry*

Contents

Somebody's murdered Manchester and not told me. Somebody's taken it to the dogs – ripped from it a history.

All is as all shouldn't be.

And here's another one of those signs – 'Thank G.B. for "The Nocturnes"' – weeping with damp . . .

Inside The Lion, posters boast the cheapest drinks this side of a dropped half-empty in the gutter; boast hot pies also. But I won't be having one of them. Leave the solids for others, I'm a liquid man today . . .

Phoenix 2006: Desert Storm!

I sensed it long before it happened.

They reminded me of the recent England team: the Beckham generation; that lot that fucked up so spectacularly in 2006 because they couldn't do what they were paid to do; because they couldn't spend time away from their birds; that lot who couldn't stop crying.

Lads with no guts, I can't stand them . . .

You're out there in America playing music, free drink, women, scenery; and you bail out in the middle of the night after the third gig.

They'd only been there for a week.

I know fellows – so-called scally types – who'd have given their right arm to be in their position. Imagine what other people think of you when they're sat at home on the dole or sat in the pub and in walks this daft guitarist who didn't have the mettle to hang in there and see the rest of America.

I thought it was hilarious when Ben Pritchard did that interview with Anthony Meirion for the unofficial Fall website, blabbing his heart out. It reminded me of one of those memoirs that politicians love writing: *Ben Pritchard: The Fall Years, 2001–2006* . . .

I think he's going through this phase at the moment where his tolerance for alcohol has just dropped . . . He's getting drunk really quickly . . . He was falling asleep in the dressing room five minutes before we were due onstage . . . when you're drunk and in a deep sleep you're not gonna get up for anyone, y'know . . . he's threatened to stab people before for waking him up, y'know.

Interview with Ben Pritchard 12 June 2006
http://www.visi.com/fall/news/pritchardint2006.html

I knew it was coming. I knew they didn't have the nerve.

Three days in and they've got faces like vexed tomatoes, their skins flaking sci-fi style: burnt to fuck. They were an embarrassment; not only to me and the wife and The Fall fans but to their own generation.

We wanted to do it and we were prepared to do it and we were looking forward to it but we knew that it was gonna be . . . it was five weeks and that's longer than we've ever done on tour with this line-up. There was already rifts and things happening when we did the last UK tour.

It's a brutal let-down for a lot of people. They go on tour and it isn't what they expected. All at once their lives don't work any more. They're adrift in more ways than they can handle. It's not for everyone; twelve-hour drives starting first thing in the morning, different food, different culture and all that shit, but it's not as if we're living in the 40s; most kids should be used to all that nowadays.

I seriously think there's something wrong with Ben. I've always suspected it. He has a stunning ability for getting the wrong end of the stick all the time about everything. I think it has something to do with him being boiled alive as a kid. There was a kettle boiling on a stove when he was four or five, and it fell on him. He had to go to hospital. I don't think his nerves have recovered. That's my theory, anyway.

We were using the Winnebago as a dressing room when we played in Tucson at the Congress Hotel and we'd been sat waiting for him and we were getting all edgy . . . you wonder what kinda mood is he gonna turn up in. Who's he gonna go for tonight? Whose turn is it? For the first two nights I was golden bollocks. It was Steve and Spen. 'You're shit, you're shit, him and me are the professionals . . .'

And at this gig in Tucson, he walked into the dressing room just in a really fucking stinking black mood. He took a bottle of wine out the dressing room, 'What the fuck you looking at? What are you fucking looking at?!' . . . And he just lifted his hand up and he's got a corkscrew in his hand. And Spence had to grab him . . . we all kinda got out of the van and we left him in there to stew. I think somebody had told him that we'd all had a meeting about him and about his behaviour, y'know, you couldn't go for a piss without somebody telling Mark and everything we did angered him. And we just wanted to get on with our jobs and we weren't being allowed to do that.

He's like an old-fashioned gentleman fraud: semi-middle class. Cooks for his parents every Tuesday – chilli; goes to church once a month. Keeping up appearances. He makes me out to be some Dennis Wheatley horror character. Telling stories of how I'd wait for them on their days off in the hotel lobby, skulking. Then I'd jump out and ask if they've had anything to eat. That's so Ben, that. I'd be having a drink in the lobby and they'd walk in and I'd ask them if they'd eaten, if they fancied a drink, if they were alright. Not in a motherly way – a simple question, basically. Nothing serious.

We were driving down from Tucson to Phoenix, driving through the desert at 70 miles an hour, we're in a Winnebago, or that kind of thing, nobody's got a seatbelt on in the back . . . And Mark was pissed . . . and he just came wandering over, walking to the front of the bus and I was sat next to the driver with a map, giving this guy directions. You know, for some reason, Mark had made this guy the enemy. Before this guy has a chance to do his job, Mark was like, 'You're fuckin' shit! I'm getting rid of him!' But he doesn't just sack him, he winds him up . . . Mark had a bottle of beer and I think he just poured a bit on this guy's head . . . some people having a beer over their head could've gone off the road, just panicked, y'know, and with people walking around in the back, he could have killed everybody . . . And he walked up to the back of me with a lit cigarette in his hand and I could smell something burning and I'm sure he was at it with a cigarette at the back of my head, just cos I was helping this guy with directions.

Tell him anything and he construes it in a paranoid way. I feel sorry for him.

I did spill some beer over the driver. I did flick a bit of paper at him; because he was asleep. Why say things like that? Why's he talking behind my back about me taking speed? It's not as if I'm jacking up every day.

He's not the first. They enter a completely different world when they join The Fall. When they're first in the group they're just used to having a few pints on the weekend, then they see me with the double whiskys. Next minute they're on the double whiskys, pint and a line of coke.

I remember Ben leaving his passport at home when we were trying to get visas sorted out. A good friend of mine had to drive back from London to Bury because Ben hadn't the spine to admit he didn't fancy the journey. He must have thought I was daft.

He talks like he was my counsellor – implies that I needed him to be my friend, but he didn't want to be burdened by me. It wasn't the case at all. I'd just talk to him because he was there. When he said I told him I'd been followed by the MI5, I told him that in jest, like a kid. Just to keep him chatting.

He thinks he knows me better than I know myself. I needed *him*? The only thing I needed him for aside from playing the guitar was to chauffeur Elena to Tesco's every now and again.

That's why I'm gutted, because I don't have anybody to call on to do that any more.

I confide more in the Post Office than Ben. That's where he gets his name from, the Bible – Benjamin, the judge.

The other daft cunt, Steve Trafford (bass), was one of Ben's mates. He appeared out of nowhere. Wouldn't tell you anything about anything; the sort who wanted to know everything about you, though, like some bored suburban housewife.

I don't think he ever wanted to be in the band anyway. I kept hearing stories about how he preferred to save his best tunes for his own band. He was never a Fall member; not in the true Fall sense.

He started losing it when it he met that actress out of *Shameless*, Maxine Peake. He didn't realize she was only hanging around with him because he was in The Fall. I found it quite amusing when she buggered off after Phoenix.

Same thing happened to Ben as well. He had this bird he couldn't stop gabbing on about, how she was this and that, and they were going to move in together, blardy-blah. Day after he's got home, he finds out she doesn't want to see him any more. That's the Curse of The Fall for you.

What annoyed me most about Steve, though, was he was always very quick to sulk. I don't like lads who are so ready to fold. And he was one of those pseudo-intellectuals as well; thinking he's bright reading *Crime and Punishment* on the tour bus, not realizing that everybody reads it at the age of fifteen. The funniest thing was, he must have been influenced by it, because he said he was going to give me a good hiding in the dressing room, just before they did their midnight flit. Imagine! I can remember him telling a story about how he stood and watched his mates get a good kicking off a bunch of kids and did fuck all about it.

The thing about the final stooge, Spencer Birtwhistle, is he's a Hacienda casualty; and not only that, he's a drummer as well. That's his background. I know for a fact he knew he'd made a mistake following Ben and Trafford out of America. He's easily led, you see. Necked too many Es. He's not as sharp as he should be.

There's a whole bunch of those people in Manchester: the living dead. Some essential trigger ceased functioning back when The Happy Mondays had another night out around 1992. I feel sorry for them. They get so caught up in a version of themselves, it becomes an unmanageable reality. The annoying thing is I helped him out by having him back in the group and he stabbed me in the back.

It was inevitable. There was something in the air there. I knew it was coming. They'd been acting like irked union members for weeks. Ben talks about how they recorded all these great tracks in Lincolnshire, just before the tour. They recorded shit – a few lame incarnations of what they thought The Fall should sound like. It was like a Sunday-before-work, been-drinking-all-weekend karaoke-take on *Fall Heads Roll*. It had no zip to it. I'm amazed he has the audacity to even mention it. It all ties in with his dust-ridden view of the music industry – being a Led Zeppelin and Pink Floyd fan. 'The great lost album' – what a load of shit!

They were losing it. And, what's more, they knew it and couldn't handle it. It's not as if they've gone on to form a supergroup; same with the other ex-members. Give them a couple of years and then it'll really set in. Mistakes like that fester.

The irony of that whole period is that Elena, the wife, was more of a man than any of them. That's always been the case. She didn't cave in. She took a lot on after they fucked off with the money, the van and the driver.

The more I look back on that whole debacle, the more I

get the feeling it was meant to be. Sometimes that's all there is to it.

But the support band didn't help, The Talk. They were like the Yank equivalent of Ben and co., soft lads with rock and roll exteriors. I think they found their soulmates in each other. And after the incident with the banana, when one of The Talk invaded the stage and whacked me on the side of the head with a banana, inside I reckon they were wishing that that had been one of them. They were all in it together. I'm something they could never be and they didn't like it.

I'm surprised they don't have any respect for their own history. Imagine looking back in ten, twenty, thirty years' time and remembering what happened over there – it's pathetic. I'd like to see them at war. It's a generational thing – something's amiss with too many lads these days around the ages of thirty-five and under. Empty of wonder. I think they've been told too much by their parents, they're not in this life to discover things for themselves.

They should go back and start their lives anew.

I feel very privileged to have been part of that group . . . most people don't last two or three years . . . for the first year you're golden bollocks. For the second year you're a piece of shit. By the third year you're accepted. You're in. And then he kind of eases up on you . . . The Fall has been my only job for a good four years now, so when we walked away from that tour it wasn't just something we did just like that, we sat and thought about it and it was the only thing we could have done. That tour, in hindsight, was a good one and it wouldn't have been if we'd have stayed . . . we just sat down and it was like, 'How much more can we put up with?'

Aftermath

I didn't really know what I was going to do. But I wasn't going home. I was determined to stick this one out. It's always the same with British bands in America: the whole work-and-play ethic turns them upside down; and then they crumble. The Yanks love it; they're sick of all that Oasis shit – do you think the Gallaghers could get a job in an American group? They couldn't even make it past New York! Have you noticed that about Oasis, they're always trying to conquer America, but never make it past New Jersey! Not only that but the Brits think they invented rock and roll. This is what pisses Americans off as well: the idea that nothing came before The Stones and Led Zeppelin; forgetting that it originated in America with Bo Diddley and Elvis.

In retrospect, it couldn't have worked out any better. The Lord provided . . . Narnack, the record company we're signed to in America, sorted us out with a new band. They got in touch with this fellow from LA, this drummer called Orpheo McCord. He, in turn, contacted his mate Rob Barbato, a bass player; and he got in touch with his band-mate and guitarist Tim Presley.

They're a solid bunch of lads. There's no ego-glorification there, none of that smelling each other's armpits and adoring each other.

Orpheo's good because he's a complete professional. Simple. He's the polar opposite to that clichéd drummer type. He put a lot of hours into the *Reformation Post-TLC* album, and didn't complain.

Rob's the same. He can play quite a few instruments as well, so he's handy to have around. He knows how to balance that drink-and-work thing too – which is rare in music.

I found it quite amusing that Ben felt compelled to mention

Rob's beard and how, in his time, I used to make everybody have a shave. I used to make them have a shave because they couldn't even grow proper stubble; they looked like a bunch of school kids trying to buy beer with bum fluff for ID. I wasn't having that.

You don't meet many guitarists like Tim, who don't sulk and think they're the centre of the universe. I never have, anyway. So clichéd. I've never met a guitarist I like really. He's alright though – he's just got an old case and an old guitar and he's not fussed about his equipment. It's not 'me, me, me' all the time with him. I think he's more of an artist. I've never heard anybody play like him, I must say that. In truth, I'm amazed how it panned out. They're the best we've had in quite a while. What's good about them is you can say, 'Can' – the old German group – and they say, 'Yeah, we like that.' Their heads aren't fogged like a lot of British groups, obsessing about U2 or The Stone Roses. They're open. You can put ideas to them and they'll say, 'Well, we've never thought of that, but we'll try it.' It's good to have a group like that. I can throw up ideas I've been thinking about for ages and not have to worry about them being interpreted in a cack-handed fashion. It frees me up.

You can hear it on *Reformation*. There's a lot more going on than you think. It was intended as a parody of Manchester groups, but turned, remarkably, into a piece of solid music. The weird bits were deliberate – maybe they got out of hand a little. The lyrics mostly I'd been keeping back from the old line-up.

I can see how people approached it as another bitter and twisted Mad Mark album, considering the climate of the period it was put together in. But, strangely enough, it began as a personal album; the events of the times led it down another path. As it should be. Some things start off one way and then spiral elsewhere.

In the end it came together like a collage: bits here, bits there. I see it as part of a trio of LPs – *Real New Fall*, *Fall Heads Roll*

and *Reformation*. There's a lineage there of sorts, a moving on.
You've got the build-up – the comeback album – and then
you've got the *settled* middle, and then the obliteration.

I've seen it all before.

It won't be long before the vampires start talking again about
things going to my head. I can hear them now.

1. The Power of my Childhood Days

When I was five I used to go and sit with my next-door neighbour, Stan the pigeon guy, in his back garden. He was a Teddy Boy, and in those days, before everyone had phones, the Teds used to send pigeons off to their girlfriends in Blackpool or wherever, with little messages attached.

Sometimes he'd have three pigeons, each with a girl's name on it. I'd say to him, 'Why you doing that, Stan?'

'So at least one of them will get through.'

Meaning that one of the pigeons would get there and come back with a message to meet a girl in Blackpool or New Brighton – First World War style.

When desperate he'd send four pigeons out, and only two would get there because the other two would have been shot down with an air rifle.

His mother was like our auntie, but she wasn't related, though it was always 'Auntie Hilda'. When I was about fifteen I asked how exactly Auntie Hilda was related to us, and my mam just said, 'She's not related to us at all, neither's Stan.' But when you're five or six you don't know these things.

I used to have Irish 'aunties' as well. They were people you could go and talk to and have a cup of tea with, not child molesters or anything, nice people – war widows, mostly.

There was a lot of pretence floating around; not just with aunties and all that but with emotions and how people saw you. They had a point. There's a lot to learn from that generation – the stoic approach. I think it's disgusting how they've been forgotten about in this way. It's the American hippies' fault, they saw an in there, a way of making money out of bad moods. That's all it is most of the time. You can't expect to feel cock-a-hoop every minute of every day. My mam and dad's generation understood this. They were just thankful the bombs had stopped threatening their lives. They just wanted to get on with living.

I liked primary school, but I didn't have any friends there. I was the only Manchester City fan in the class, everybody else was United. I set a long-jump record as well; it still exists, I think. That was a major achievement at the time.

One of the funniest incidents that happened to me when I was a kid was when I went to the premiere of *Zulu* in Whitefield with my dad. I was only five or so. One of my relations had been at Rorke's Drift: 'Hooky', the skiver. James Booth played him in the film. He was a relation of my dad's.

It's an embarrassment to the family actually. My dad was there in his overalls – he didn't know what was going on. We had to sit in this big special box. And there were relations of relations of relations in these four other boxes; all boring bastards shouting at the screen, 'There's my great-grandfather – Officer Bromhead': the Michael Caine character with the cut-glass accent and the brand-new uniform. And I'm going, 'Dad, which one are we related to?' And there he is on the screen, pissed, laid up in bed; on the skive with a boil on his arse. The thing was, my dad was a soldier and my mam's dad was too. It wasn't very nice for them seeing this. Hooky wasn't that bad, though. He was quite a brave man. He was a proletarian soldier. He'd been in the army a long time and he was just trying to keep himself alive. He had a lot of sense; if you watch the film, he tells people to stay where they are instead of wearing a red tunic and walking out and getting shot. Most of them hadn't seen combat before.

Queen Victoria looked after all those fellows. Nobody liked it because she insisted that they get four quid every year or something. And if they died then the relatives would get it. She insisted they all got Christmas cards and money for a long time afterwards. Do you think the government is sending money to the families of kids from Bury who've died out there in Iraq?

Worst thing was, when I was about six I went blind. I had an eye disease that nobody could understand. I just woke up one morning and everything looked like it was in Hebrew or Greek. It's like being thrown into a foreign country. Teachers said I was skiving: 'You could read last year so why can't you read now, you're playing the donkey.' That's what they used to call me.

For half a year everything looked upside down, like ancient letters, hieroglyphics. My mam, God bless her, went to the doctor but he said, 'He's just putting it on.' Hospital said the same.

But she was very persistent: took me to a specialist, which was hard in those days, because she didn't have any money. And he said, 'I can't see anything wrong.' She went everywhere.

Her argument was that he could read when he was five, so why not now?

Eventually she went to a clinic in Prestwich, and there was a matron there. They don't have these places any more, it was called a local clinic and you could just walk in. This matron said I'd got a lazy eye. That's all it was. I had to wear a big patch for two months. But these people were talking about eye surgery, and taking me to a home for people with reading disabilities. My mam was having none of it. It was terrifying. One year you're as good as anybody else in the class, if not better, then in the new term you can't even write 'the'.

You find out who your friends are in those circumstances. I distinctly remember everybody stopped talking to me at school. It didn't bother me, because I had a lot of Irish mates who didn't give a fuck about reading or writing. I used to stay with this Irish family in Salford. They were helping my mam and dad out. They were lovely people. Always singing Elvis songs and these old Dublin ballads. But they never knew the lyrics, they'd just make them up. Their version of 'All the Young Dudes' was fantastic, better than the original – 'I'm going to Woolworths, I'm going to shag a cow to death . . .'. Proper lyrics.

In a way, as a result, I skipped out on the eight-to-ten period, when teachers really start to influence you.

I wasn't really into girls either. I couldn't even stand my sisters. Sometimes in the school holidays when I was about twelve, and my mam and dad were at work, I'd be looking after five fucking girls: my three sisters, this adopted kid, and another whose parents were abusive to her. They were about four or five at the time.

I devised this thing called 'Japanese prison camp'. I'd make them sit in this room under a table with a big cloth over them because the air force might be coming. I'd be the Japanese guard. 'You can't go out. You must stay under there,' I'd tell them. Then I'd shut the door, say I was going to the bridge on the River Kwai, have some pop, go out with my mates and, half an hour before my mam and dad came home, I'd return, saying, 'Japanese prison camp is now over.'

If they escaped, the punishment would be 'No lemonade'. They used to love it. Throw sweets under the cloth. Good laugh.

Occasionally I'd let a couple escape. I'd leave the back door open. They liked that: running around the back garden. Then I'd lock the doors and they'd be pleading to get back to the prison camp. 'You'll have to wait for your mam to come home,' I'd say.

They always remember it, my sisters, when they get a bit pissed: 'We remember Japanese prison camp, you don't fool us, you pop star.' And my mam's going, 'What's Japanese prison camp?' Today we'd probably get investigated by the social services. What can you do? It's hard work bringing up kids. Japanese prison camp was the perfect solution.

Sometimes it comes out, though, like with their ex-husbands who say, 'I blame us splitting up because of the way you treated them.' And I'll go, 'What you talking about?' And they're like, 'I've heard the stories about Japanese prison camp.'

The other game was Auntie Nowty. Our aunties never used to come round, so I'd say, 'Your auntie's coming round and you have to wait for her.' They'd all get dressed up. And I'd bang on the stairs with my mam's shoes, like in *Psycho*. And they'd go, 'Mark, what's going on?' and I'd say, 'It's your auntie, your Auntie Nowty – she's got a bad temper – you've got to be very well behaved.' And leave them in their room. Go downstairs, read my dad's paper, look at the racing and football results. And then they'd start screaming and run out, asking where she is. I'd say she's very nowty, she's gone to town without you, she's sick of waiting for you. They were safe, weren't they? You couldn't have them roaming around the streets.

I was one of those weird kids that passed their 11-plus but still wanted to go to school with my friends. St Joey's Secondary Modern School – it had one of the worst academic records in the whole of Britain. You had a choice. When you were fourteen or fifteen it was your choice, not like now; it's all about the parents now.

But I ended up at Stand Grammar all the same.

Twelve going on sixty, that's what people used to say about me; a twelve-year-old wanting to be a sixty-year-old man.

I couldn't stand music when I was that age. I hated it, thought it was vaguely effeminate. I remember seeing Peter Noone and pictures of Black Sabbath, believe it or not, which sort of got me intrigued. But I wasn't that bothered. Most of my mates were into soul and James Brown. I didn't mind a bit of Northern Soul; but nothing else really.

Music to me was something your sisters did. My three sisters all had posters of Cliff and the Osmonds over the house. I was more into causing trouble, forming gangs and things like that. I used to have a few – Psycho Mafia, the Barry Boy gang. We'd fight other gangs. It was quite interesting; there used to be Irish gangs and Orthodox Jewish gangs. But the Psycho Mafia was a real melting pot, and I was the vice president.

If there was somebody from another gang on the same paper round from another newsagents we used to set his papers on fire. Or put notes inside saying, 'Piss off missus – your paper boy!' Things like that, little things.

We had a camp in St Mary's park, Prestwich – a little tent behind some trees, where we'd put knocked-off Kit-Kats and Lion bars, and copies of *Playboy*; made a lot of money flogging porn mags, selling them to the suckers behind the bike-sheds. The Irish lads would be like, 'Who the hell wants to look at some woman with no clothes on, I can see it every day with me sister?' But the fuckers would still buy them. We used to sell it per page. But *Playboy* was quite literary in those days, so some kids would say, 'Have you got them four pages of *Playboy*?' And the front page would be a Playboy bunny, and the other three pages an interview with Norman Mailer: 'His Life in Question', or 'Hunting and Fishing in Nevada'. Sometimes we'd even substitute it with pages from *Woman's Own*, some romance story.

I feel deeply sorry for a lot of kids nowadays. They're missing out on things. I walk the streets at 11.15 at night when you can't get a cab, through the so-called rough areas like Cheetham Hill, and it's so quiet. But you couldn't do that when I was a kid because there were so many gangs around, more than there are today. But there's something sad about this false idea of kids being outside – if they're out they're going to hit you or mug you. It's a consolidated effort by the government. That computer trick's the best one – every house should have a computer for the kids! It's ridiculous, it's like brain damage. When I was younger it was everybody should have a book to read – 'Harold should have a book to read every day.' And lads would be at home just staring at this thing, this book; and they're not reading it at all, probably having a wank instead; which saved the government work, and the police, because they're inside – much like today with 'Every home should have a computer.'

When I was twelve, thirteen, I was into reading imported American comics. It's a good visual medium for a kid, comics. But now you see them with their daft computer games – running through mazes. It's soulless, zapping people; makes Desperate Dan and Dennis the Menace look great, like modern art.

I was never a TV person either. I'd be upstairs. My mam and dad never watched it either. This was the time when TV was coming in. We were the only country in the world that took it that seriously in the 60s and 70s. It was like a family ritual, with everybody sitting on the couch. But not in my family.

As for school – Stand Grammar – I never really liked it. My main ambition when I was fourteen was to get out. I just wanted to sign on. Couldn't understand these lads and girls who wanted to stay around and be told what to do. I just wanted my own place. You could do that then, sign on and live, but not now.

I started writing around that time as well, when I was fourteen, fifteen. I wasn't particularly influenced by anybody, just used to write short stories and little pieces to amuse myself.

I spent a lot of time in the library. Solitude. I was living in a small house with six or seven other people. It never bothered me much, really. But it's the same as when I go on stage – I need to carve out my own space now and again. I can happily sit on a bus with twelve people, that's the way I've been brought up. But if I'm doing anything, I need room.

The thing about school was, I couldn't get my head around any of the prescribed books – *The Hobbit*, for instance. The master used to read us *The Hobbit* – can you believe it? That's all we used to talk about – small men in holes. We had a protest about it, against him. He used to room with J. R. R. Tolkien, and that's all he'd ever talk about, his days with J.R.R. The prefects actually backed us up; because we were saying this is supposed to be English literature and we're reading this shit, this fairy story, when we're supposed to be reading Shakespeare and medieval poetry.

I liked Thomas Hardy's *The Mayor of Casterbridge*. I did that for my O level; great book.

Another thing I objected to was the way they tried to tell you which university to go to, or if you didn't want that, they already had a job worked out for you when you were thirteen or fourteen. For instance, I was a two-O-level boy who was supposed to go and get a job in Kendal's, or if not that then go and work in the Civil Service or the army. Unbelievable.

Outside of school there were always the cider gangs and all that. But all my mates were Irish, and they didn't really drink. I like that about the Irish with their kids – they're dead strict. There was always a big lock on the drinks cabinet.

My mam wouldn't even let me take an aspirin. I appreciate that now. She had it around, but she'd be like, 'No, not for you.' It's that wartime-generation thing, where you've got to be bleeding to death before you get aspirin. I remember being at school when I was eleven and the kids would have aspirin in their pockets to take during the day if they got a headache, but I never had anything like that.

I started smoking when I was about sixteen. I don't think you need it really before then. I couldn't see the point to it. You can't appreciate it then. We used to write our names on walls and garages with Capstan Full Strength cig-ends; they were that strong, like black chalk; better than a pen.

I took acid before I had a packet of cigarettes in fact, at fifteen. I was on acid before I even had any pot; pot was for hippies. I had no problem with the acid because it was proper LSD. I remember my sister giving me a copy of 'I Can Hear the Grass Grow' by The

Move; a second-hand copy. And I listened to it on acid. Couldn't believe it – knocks all that other psychedelic shit into touch. 'Night of Fear' is a good record too; with that bit from Tchaikovsky in it. Apparently, Carl Wayne, who was the frontman, hadn't a clue what he was singing about. (He married Diane out of *Crossroads* afterwards as well.)

If anything, I was doing acid to get away from the cider clubs and the sherry clubs. Kids of about fourteen used to nick their mam's 'British Sherry' and be sick all over the house. You could tell where they lived by the drink and vomit stains on the carpet. But the bikers were doing a lot of acid, and I was vaguely connected to that scene. My sisters had boyfriends who were bikers. And around Victoria Station there were a lot of biker pubs. And the bikers, of course, wouldn't wear helmets – this was a big deal; so they're getting stopped all the time for drink driving. And they've all seen *Easy Rider*, so they're all shoving big tabs of acid down their throats with half a pint of Tetley's, and I mean real acid. Uncontaminated.

Imagine being on a motorbike on acid . . . I suppose it concentrated your mind. You knew where you were going – safe as houses in that Robert Crumb land; faces coming at you, red lights. Look at the pavement and it's like a snake. You weren't out of your head though, you just felt like the Master Race.

That was my ambition at the time: get a flat, take drugs, and not work. But I needed to be earning. My dad never gave me any money. I used to go to work with him in the summer holidays. Everybody else would be out playing or doing whatever, and I'd be cleaning toilets and drains out. I remember sweeping up and hearing The Move and The Kinks on the radio; good education.

My dad was very tough: a hard-case. Not in a violent way, but mentally. It must have been hard for him. I appreciate it now, though. He reminds me of the copper in *Life on Mars*, the Gene Hunt character. He's great, that fellow. It's a fantastic representation of that sort of bloke – there's a reason why that show's doing so well. Characters like that were quite fair-minded in their own way. I'm not saying they're a perfect type, just that they have a lot of instinctive common sense.

I remember meeting a girl when I was about thirteen or fourteen – Sharon, she was called. Met her at Radcliffe bus station. She was with this other girl and I was with a mate of mine. We ended up in a barn somewhere. My mate's getting into this girl, and I'm sheepishly kissing Sharon. Anyway, a few days later, there's a knock at the door. Sunday afternoon this was, we've just had our tea, my mam answers the door, and there's Sharon and her mam; pair of them all dressed up. I couldn't believe it. My dad wanted them out. He just kept saying, 'Get 'em out!' But my mam's not like that. She sat them down with a cup of tea and cake.

I had to go out the back with Sharon. We walked around while they all had a talk about me and her . . . but my dad was having none of it. He didn't want to see me stuck with this girl from Radcliffe who I'd only just met. I didn't even want to be with her. But her mam thought we made a really good couple. Like mams do sometimes . . . When they finally got rid of them, my dad took me to one side and asked me what I'd been up to and all that. I hadn't been up to anything, and I told him that.

I think they had the right idea back then. You see dads nowadays, always hanging around their kids. It's ridiculous. It's more about them than the kids, their ideas. My dad worked all day and he'd be out at night. But that's how it was in those days.

When I was on tour in the early days I used to ring my dad up and ask him to collect the mail, and he'd be like, 'What are you doing?'

'I'm in Germany.'

'What you doing there?'

'Doing very well.'

'You must be mad.'

Because he saw Germany as just a load of old women walking round with sticks and a load of rubble; still thinking it's 1946.

'Is this what it's come to?' he'd say.

I used to love it. I'd tell the other fellows and they'd go, 'I'd cry if my father said that to me.' But I used to piss myself.

I'd say to him, 'Well, it's 1979, Dad, things have changed a bit.' And his answer would always be, 'You can kid your mam but you can't kid me.'

He never really understood why I was doing it. Better that than those other dads picking you up at the airport when you're thirty-one! Like Steve Trafford's dad, asking how many people turned up and how much money we'd made.

I couldn't even afford to go to college; went for about three months but I never had any money. Looking back, I never liked college anyway, I educated myself better. But my dad was good like that. His philosophy was – 'Look, if you've got a fiver in your pocket on a Friday night you're made.' Real English working class – what you once thought of as a handicap comes in really useful later on when you're down on your luck or the band's got no money. I'll never forget that.

2. Grandad versus King Kong

Fred, my grandad, was a real pragmatist. He had a big plumbing shop in Salford near Strangeways Prison on this green hillock. Eighteen apprentices. His idea of a good time was reading a book on plumbing, on how to dispose of shit.

He'd stand outside Strangeways and recruit ex-prisoners, get them making lathes and pipes. At the time they were recruiting for the army and he'd say, 'You've got a choice, you either go to Ireland or you come with me.'

I used to sit around with all these blokes who'd just been released from prison. I bump into them when I'm in Manchester sometimes. Fellows who are about fifty-five. They just come up and say, 'You're Fred's grandson, aren't you?' and I'll be thinking, 'Oh fucking hell, what they going to say now?' But they're really complimentary, they say things like, 'Your grandad met me outside Strangeways one Wednesday afternoon, and he turned my life around.'

Different times then, different people, unlike the ungrateful musicians I employ. They say that there's a generation gap: you're not actually like your mam and dad, you're more like your grandfather or grandmother. You skip a generation. In this respect I had more in common with my grandad than I did with my dad – just hiring people off the street. If they go, they go, if they don't, they don't. I'm not really bothered where people come from.

My grandad would hang around the cinema and say to his apprentices, 'Look, lad, your brain will turn to water watching that.' He didn't like the idea of people wasting their time, and back then the big source of entertainment was the cinema.

He had a particular grudge against *King Kong*. He was seriously worried about it, people staring at this big monkey that didn't even look real. I like that. I understand where he's coming from, in a way. Not that I'm against watching films. It's more the idea that you can kid yourself too much. To be honest, it's probably more relevant today than it was then. Now when you go to the cinema you've got to be dead silent. It's bollocks. People actually believe what they're watching. I remember when I used to go and watch films with my Irish mates as a kid, we'd be yelling at the screen, at Dracula with all this blood on his chin, which was obviously tomato sauce or whatever; it was more of an experience then. There'd always be a *Carry On* film on every Saturday around Prestwich and Salford and Manchester; for the dirty old men. We used to get thrown out when Sid James came on; thrown out after about five minutes – because they were shit. Holiday-camp shit. My Irish mates would be shouting out, 'This is the bit where Sidney puts his hand up the girl's skirt!' And we'd get thrown out!

I'd prefer to see a good film, like Albert Finney in *Charlie Bubbles*, or *Dead of Night*. But now you get the BBC with their *Carry On* seasons! It's trash! The *Beano* was better.

I can't go in the cinema now. I went to see *The Blair Witch Project* with my sister. Ten minutes in, I'm going, 'Ohh, this is scary!': joking. People were turning around telling me to be quiet. After about half an hour I'm saying it's a home movie, it's not a horror film.

Whatever you say about Hammer Horror films, at least everybody used to have a good laugh. I used to watch them and go 'Aaarrgghh!' when Dracula appeared. If you did that now you'd be booted out, people take it so seriously. When characters used to get shot, we'd shout out, 'That's a lot of tomato ketchup, that!' and the audience would laugh. Nowadays people think it's art. Hammer Horror films never pretended to be art. It was what it was; nothing wrong with that. It served its purpose.

I can't believe they remade *The Omen*, though, that's a great film. You watch it and think, 'Right, he's had it, he's in for it now, just wait . . .' Brilliant.

There's a dearth of original scripts, that's why Hollywood has to remake everything. The only one I didn't mind was *The Manchurian Candidate*; not as good as the original, but there was something there.

Nothing touches *Dead Man's Shoes*, though. British film – set in Nottingham. Not many people have heard of it, because it isn't your average idea of Britain. It's not *Notting Hill* or Hugh Grant, and it's not even Mike Leigh or Ken Loach. It doesn't patronize or meander and it's not afraid to tell a story. I like the way it captures Britain in the summertime, when some people don't have enough money to go on holiday and they spend most of their time drinking or doing drugs: walling themselves off. There's a lot of frustration there; it doesn't help when they're seeing their bosses and workmates fucking off on another holiday. You can see it in the pubs; men who've been out all day in the sun with big red faces that you could fry an egg on, bruised complexions – looking at you . . .

You could go in The Forresters – a pub near me – and nobody would look at you ten years ago. It wasn't the way they were thinking. But now they feel they've got to look at you. I've seen people, heard people in pubs, saying, 'That guy over there – he's weird.' They're not weird. You're weird: a grown man looking at everybody else. Fellows are worse than the women.

One thing that shocked me when I first went to Europe was the way in which Dutch people and French people used to stare at you. I found it very offensive. Not because of who I was; but because it was an incursion on my space. It just didn't used to happen in Britain. The strange thing now is that it's not just old people; it used to be an old person's game – looking. Not now, though. All ages are into it.

Things like *Big Brother* I find very strange. Why should anyone want to watch somebody asleep at night? Now that's weird. They asked me to replace Johnny Rotten on *I'm a Celebrity Get Me Out of Here*. I'd never dream of doing anything like that. He must have been seriously broke to have even considered it. But that's his business. Programmes like that remind me of wartime Russia when they'd make so-called subversive artists dig holes and plough fields. It's very sad: every year at a certain time *we* get to have a laugh at celebrities who are skint or desperate or just simply mad. The worst part about it is that kids watch it; that's the last thing I'd be doing as a kid. I would never have dreamed of wasting my time like that. Though I must confess I sometimes do it now, spend days watching the TV knowing I should be getting on with something else – it gets like a drug. I remember one year when I watched nothing but *Dallas* – it was great. JR: fantastic. Didn't mind *Dynasty* either. Me and Elena like *Neighbours* as well; Doctor Carl, he's great. I particularly liked that band he had at one stage. Good band: good TV.

But as a kid I had more on my mind. I wanted to engage with my surroundings, do things. Nowadays everybody's just looking at everybody else. I don't care. I don't care how much so and so earns a week. It's not my business. Something happened around 1997. All of a sudden we're interested in tittle-tattle. All of a sudden people are making money out of tittle-tattle – I'm talking about the *Big Brother* mindset here. Suddenly from doing interviews about how I came by lyrics, and why am I obsessed with horror, and why does this album sound like that, blardy-blah; to how often do you have sex a week? Or, what's your favourite LP? *What's your favourite LP?* – who *cares*? They're supposed to be journalists, aren't they? That's not my idea of a proper journalist.

I heard a story the other day about some daft fellow naming his kid Keegan after Kevin Keegan. If I'd have told my dad or grandad about that, they'd have said, 'Stop hanging around with people like that. You should get away from people like that.' I mean, how stupid is that? Naming your son Keegan . . . Now that's tittle-tattle gone too far. What sort of mentality is that?

It's a shame that people are living their lives like this, because it goes much quicker than you think. I'd rather people concentrated on their own ideas a bit more. It's as if they don't think their own lives are of any importance; completely different from people of my dad and grandad's generation, who at least had an understanding of what it was to exist, to try and do things and not waste time.

When I formed the group it wasn't about me trying to get my picture in some paper or magazine or other – like it is with a lot of bands nowadays – it was because of sounds; of wanting to make something; combining primitive music with intelligent lyrics.

You've got to realize and accept that you're never going to be on *Top of the Pops* every week if you're in The Fall, that's not what The Fall's about; The Fall's about hard work. At the time I wasn't conscious of this but later on I soon recognized that this was what it was about. You can't be flaky about these things. You have to face up to it. There have been many times I've thought about packing it in and going off to do something else. I've always wanted to write a really good British film – something on a par with *Dead of Night*. But I've never quite got there. Other things have got in the way.

3. Prelude to Revolution

They used to have job agencies in those days, these bureaus. You'd just walk in and say, 'I'm sixteen, got five O levels, get us a job.' And they would. Imagine that now. If you got sacked you could just get another job. They were great like that, and they were free. So this bureau sent me to this meat factory to deal with the clerical work. It was the biggest meat-processing plant in Manchester, owned by Louis Edwards, who owned everything from Cheetham Hill to Victoria Station, every factory.

So Martin, his son, who later became the Chairman of Manchester United, walked in. 'You've been sent by this bureau,' he said.

'Yeah, but I don't think it's enough money. I've got offers for fourteen and fifteen quid a week, and yours is only eight and half a week.'

'Well, here's your documents, and here's your filing cabinet and you start on Monday.'

'No, Mr Edwards, I don't.'

'There's where the lorries go out, there's your packing staff, and you're in charge.'

'You don't seem to understand me; I can't do it for eight and half quid a week.'

'Well, I'll just leave you with the papers and I'll come back in half an hour.'

So I thought, alright, I'll have a look. So I start looking through the papers, and it's all about processed steaks and how many they need or don't need. Instantly, I knew it was all shit. I knew I couldn't do it.

After half an hour he hasn't come back. I thought to my-self, fuck this, I'll go to my next interview – which you could do in those days. But I couldn't open the door. So I knocked on the window with a ruler to get the attention of one of the meat packers. One of them turned around and said, 'What's wrong?'

'Fire!' I said. So this guy goes and gets a security guard, who unlocks the door; but they're like, 'What's the matter? Mr Edwards said you're the new packing clerk.' Which makes me think, because years later when he was at United it was much the same: 'You're here now, so fuck off' type of philosophy.

Though, looking back, if I'd known he was going to be head of United in years to come I wouldn't have even gone to the interview in the first place.

After that I went to the docks in Salford as a shipping clerk. They were much more free and easy. I was sixteen. People were great, working with dockers and shipping agencies. At the time it was incredible: big ships coming in from Canada, Nigeria, Ghana, full of fruit. I enjoyed my work. It was better than being at college. Got to see all sorts of people – Yanks, Nigerians, all wanting a pint as soon as they'd got off the boat – but I had to clear them, make sure all their insurance was alright.

I used to write in my lunch hour, jot things down. The docks gave me the time to do that.

But it's a good thing The Fall did happen because I got fired by this dickhead; got fired because I was a bit late. I'd been late a few times, but they'd just got this new management. Things were changing. Three-day week, candles on your desk . . . One day there's no boats from Nigeria. All of a sudden it's machine parts from Germany. We're part of the Common Market now, so the dockers were mooning about, all miserable, blaming I don't know who.

I remember having a distinct feeling that this was all going to collapse around me. One minute I'm in the office doing imports and exports; going to work in my shirt and pants, normal-like; on a motorbike, going down to the docks, earning the money – and suddenly there's these twats there in Rod Stewart suits, running the fucking company. But they had this old accountant there, about seventy, I'll never forget him: Trevor. He was like Rumpole. Smoked a pipe. He'd been in the Royal Navy fighting the Japs; and he was always telling me – 'Get out, Mark, get out now. You're too intelligent for this job.'

He used to follow me to the toilet. Asking me why I'm still here. He was looking after me.

The new manager looked like a footballer in his big pink suit; and the deputy manager like Rod Stewart. Going to the girls, 'Oh, your skirt's nice,' and all this shit. And we'd be sitting in the manager's office, and I'd be like, 'Yeah, what's the problem?' with all this stuff on my face because I'd just come from the docks. And Trevor would be there with his pipe.

And the first thing this fellow said was, 'I had the best jump of my life last night.' He'd just got married as well!

I remember Trevor looking at me, and later saying, 'Even the lowest sailor wouldn't say things like that.'

I mean, I wasn't a saint in those days, but fuck me . . . This fellow with his big suit and sun-tan. We've got two boats holed up in Salford; you could see it was going down the drain. And all he's talking about is his car, or last night's jump, or how 'things are going to change'.

They came in like New Labour – a total overhaul. It all changed – the whole office. I'm glad I witnessed that. I'd be talking to India or wherever, and they'd be asking me stupid questions like, 'Have you not done those machine parts from Switzerland yet?'

This is the new sales rep saying this; they sacked the old one, who was this bearded guy with a tweed jacket. Used to get everybody leathered, all his clients. He'd come in pissed out of his head – 'There's two boats of cloth from Nigeria sorted out' – but he'd get the contracts.

But they couldn't sack Trevor, because he only worked part-time. He used to say, 'This is what happened in Singapore, before the Japanese invaded.'

I knew I was for the push, though. They'd always be getting me on my time. Out with the old and in with the new; but what did the new do? How long did they last? Eighteen months. Every container you saw on Salford docks was owned by that company, and now it's a casino.

I went home, on the dole.

Around 1979 I rang them up for a laugh, to speak to a few old mates; one of them had seen a review in the *NME* and tried to get in touch. So I rang him back but there was nobody left.

In a strange way, I'm still very clerical about most things I do. I suppose I'm still in The Fall because it forces me to make something of myself, which in its own way is a very desk-job attitude to have. It's probably why I record so much. If it wasn't for The Fall, I'd be at home right now trying to motivate myself to write, but probably doing every other thing possible not to write. Fucking around with this and that. Going to the pub. Watching TV. It's that old writer's dilemma. Unless you're forced to work, you find yourself cleaning out the backyard as an excuse.

In my book, the more you want to make of your life, then the more you fucking do. I wonder sometimes when I look at bands what their brains must be like. Thomas Carlyle, the Scottish writer, said, 'Produce, produce – it's the only thing you're there for.' This is what I'm talking about.

I didn't mind being on the dole. I had a lot of time on my hands as a result. Other people went to university and I read books, smoked cigs and looked around most days. It's good to have a period like that in your life, when you're not being forced to think like others. Don't get me wrong, I had my fair share of dull days and my diet wasn't the most healthy . . .

The main thing was, I read a lot of good books and wrote a lot; most of which found itself on our first LP. I didn't think of it like that when I was writing. I just felt an urge to write. I'm still like that, with reading as well. I need to read a certain amount of words a day – it doesn't matter what it is; it can be a newspaper or a book. All I know is that I get very annoyed if I've not written or read anything on a particular day.

If you're a cod-psychologist I guess you could trace most of The Fall's output back to this period, to the wilderness years; the dole days; back to young Mark laying the hard foundations for the rough and brilliant years that he hasn't yet seen!

It's amazing how many books you'll read when they're not being forced on to you by some indifferent teacher. I remember reading *The Friends of Eddie Coyle* by George V. Higgins and thinking, this is what writing's all about. I ripped through that fucker in the space of days. If only they fed you books like that at school.

I never felt better than anybody though, never felt superior, in that sort of arrogantly artistic way. That's why I never really liked John Lennon. He seemed very arrogant. It was all about being an artist with him – the living part was secondary to his stance. I've never wanted to be like that. I think it's more important to be a man than it is to be an *artist*.

To certain people you've got to be a bit poetic, or a bit aggressive. They have their image of you – and I play up to it. But it's a protection, a screen. I can pull it out when I need it, because with some people you do need it.

It's hard enough to draw breath some days, never mind with some daft scourge wanting to infect me with his shit. And invariably it's a bloke. It's funny, because with people like that, who feel the need to really press themselves on you, you can see the lad they were twenty or thirty years ago in their faces.

They're disappointed with the way they've handled those years. Fuck all to do with me. I don't get it a lot but when I have I've just pulled out my other side; the malevolent Mark side – that's always been enough to see them off.

Hear the clatter of late afternoon karaoke sung by the straw-boned, soon-to-be new barmaid, and it sounds like a cat holocaust.

I wish she'd just stop; just for a minute or so . . .

4. The Phantom Nazis

I started going out with Una Baines after meeting her in Heaton Park. I moved in with her soon after. And I knew Martin Bramah through Tony Friel. I used to see him around Prestwich.

It was hell for me. It was like a semi-commune, that flat in Kingswood Road; Bramah meditating, somebody giving a lecture on vegetarianism, and Baines, my supposed girlfriend, in bed with some hippy. I wasn't in love with her though.

But you're stuck when you're on the dole, nowhere to go.

We lived at the back of the mental hospital. Una worked there. Psychiatric nurses lived in every two or three houses. Biggest mental hospital in Europe; serious mental patients. I'd invite patients in for a cup of tea. Sit them down, play them some rock and roll, a bit of telly. Sometimes I think I did more good than all the nurses put together. They'd go out all cheerful.

It was bad in those days, but I think it's just as bad now, worse. That's what the song 'Repetition' is about. They used to give them Largactyl and Mandrax for depression, heavy downers; but when you went out into the sun all your face would flare up into blisters. I took them for kicks just to see what they were like. Always been like that, experimenting. You'd be lucky if you had two pints in your local and you could make it home with half a Mandrax in you. Out of your box. Your skin feels itchy. And that was sanctioned by the National Health!

I'd say to them, 'What you in for, Terry?' or whoever it was, and he'd tell me this story of when he was eleven and he'd nicked like two bob out of his mam's purse, so they had him sectioned. And there was one woman whose mam just didn't like her. She shouted a bit too much: bunged in the mental home for fifteen years. Fellows in there from the 30s and 40s; some councillor had just decided to label them 'Mentally Ill'. Or somebody's father had died and their mam had married another fellow, who the kid didn't like − this kid obviously going through puberty − and they'd be in there for fifteen years. Terrible.

I'd take them to the pub: a bit of normality. Then I'd walk back with them, and all the nurses would be sat cross-legged on the floor, saying, 'Now, Terry, we must try some yoga.' Playing them Pink Floyd and all that. It's where my dislike of hippies came from, I think. I used to say to the girls, 'Who are the patients and who are the nurses here?' All the guys with long hair would be saying, 'Press your toes and do some acupuncture on yourself, Terry.'

Nowadays reminds me of the late 70s. It's feasible − all those people who are in power now were student nurses back then, or student lawyers. And they're now running the country with that same mentality: give him a computer, give him a few drugs. I actually think in their heads they thought they were doing the patients some good by playing them a whole Pink Floyd LP, or Tangerine Dream. I honestly do . . .

As the world progresses they always crack on that everybody will be more independent, when in fact the opposite has happened. You see adverts for computers talking about how you can chat to somebody's brain. It's impossible. In the late 70s you'd have eight to ten people from all ages sat down cross-legged communicating through Pink Floyd or group tarot readings. I wouldn't do that. They thought I was weird because I had a leather jacket on. But if you look at it now, it's only the same thing − there's still eight people in a room but they're all in front of a screen. It's a lot safer now because they can do it from their houses. But it's the same thing. Chat rooms are the new dinner parties. People thinking they're all on the same level – to me it's impossible, as it was then, with the obligatory joint, everybody thinking the same, or thinking they're thinking the same . . . No independent thought. At least in the 70s you had to get up off your arse and go and meet these people, go around to their house; discuss things, and come to some sort of agreement.

Prestwich was quite a going place in the 70s. You wouldn't believe it now. I tell it to Elena and she can't believe it. You could go in The Wilton, or The Priests Retreat as it's called now, and you could get anything you fucking wanted – acid, dope, anything. People talk about there being a lot of coke around now . . . they should have seen it then.

I was seen as a bit of an oddball in there because I had short hair and wore a leather jacket, which was quite unusual.

Me and my three sisters used to play darts in The Forresters. I would have been about sixteen, seventeen then. My dad was a fantastic darts player: dead eye. I used to be like that, could see a pin in the distance. Not now, though, my eyes are fucked now. I liked it, the atmosphere of the place. I don't think you should be allowed in a pub until you're sixteen or seventeen. It's a place for adults. You should be made to hold back on it – do other things. You'll appreciate it more later on.

The Fall just came about really, the four of us holed up in that flat, doing our thing. The punk scene had just started. So when I first saw The Pistols at the Lesser Free Trade Hall in '76, I thought, my lot are not as bad as that. We're better. We just need a drummer. I was listening to a lot of 60s garage music, like the *Nuggets* LP, The Ramones, Patti Smith, German rock. I never had any ideas for it, because I was on the docks earning money in the early days. I was into the poetry side of things. Prose, too. I never really thought of myself as a writer, though.

It was just something I did for my own amusement; still is, really.

The other three were all into Weather Report and all that: jazz fusion. I said, you're not doing that!

Strangely enough, one of the best gigs I saw in the 70s was Gary Glitter and the Glitterband. This was just before The Fall. It was astonishing. A friend of mine put a Glitter record on in a pub recently and they turned it off because of what he is now, but it's worth remembering what a great band they were. The sound was heavy, like a war tank, two drums blasting out at you. And when Glitter went off to change his outfit midway through, the drums just played out this incessant, deep rhythm like Can or something. I was stood at the back of the hall, but I could see all the girls at the front throwing their knickers at him . . . He seemed quite restrained that night in that respect. And though I'm not defending him, what a lot of people fail to realize is that the working class had a different attitude towards sex in those days, pre-Aids and pre-safe sex. There'd be hordes of girls in the park near me, and that's all they were up for. And from what I could see on that night they were literally throwing themselves at him – offering themselves up to him. And though it stands to reason what he did was wrong, it's worth considering the climate of the time and that whole scene. Kids would have done anything to have met Glitter; for a year or two he was something else.

Anyway, I was more influenced by that than the stuff Friel and Baines were listening to. It had more edge. Stevie Wonder's 'Superstition' was another. Unlike Weather Report it doesn't force its quality, it isn't false; it's very much a record that's aware of its own strengths. I like the direct poetry of its lyrics, too, the economy. Journalists ramble on about Dylan being a poet and all that, how his words have the ability to do this and that – totally overlooking stuff like 'Superstition'; probably because most of the journalists writing that stuff are white males who grew up trying to be Dylan and now can't move on from that same wave of thought.

It was me and Tony who decided to call it The Fall, after the Albert Camus book. He wanted to call it The Outsiders at first after another Camus book; but I'd read *The Outsider* and didn't particularly like it. I thought *The Fall* was a better book. But for a period of time we were The Outsiders until I found a seven-inch in Shudehill by a 60s band called The Outsiders – 'A Question of Temperature' it was called. Good record. So that meant we were The Fall.

The connotations of the name are quite strange. It works on different levels. Very religious middle-aged people see it as a comment on the fall of man. A lot of Americans see it as the autumn of rock music – serious people, not loonys. Russian fans see it as a sword of vengeance against communism.

Bramah was the singer because he had the looks, Friel was the bass player, Una had to save up for a keyboard and I played the guitar. And we got this drummer in from Stockport, this little bald man: Dave. He died actually.

A lot of mistruths have been reported about the early days. For instance, it was Bramah and Baines who used to wear the Nazi armbands when we were forming The Fall. Don't know what they thought they were doing, but I would never wear a Nazi armband. My dad would have fucking murdered me for wearing something like that. Friel was half-Jewish, and even he used to wear one. But then it got popular with The Pistols too.

I remember going into a biker pub and Bramah and Baines both had leather jackets on and Hitler Youth armbands, and I'm saying, 'Take that off!' They thought being in a biker pub they could integrate themselves by wearing these bands. They had this middle-class idea that all bikers are Nazis – which is the worst thing you could think. Bramah and Baines caused all the fights. I'd be under a table, or dragging them out because they'd ruined my chances of getting any acid. Whatever you say about the bikers, they weren't Nazis. Might be in America, but not here. They're all talking about themselves when they say I wore a Nazi armband; quite interesting really.

I'd have just two pints, maybe some acid, but they lived on a different planet. Whenever I do see them now – and it's rare – they're always apologizing for something; don't know what it is, must be what they say about me. My sister Barbara, she was a Hell's Angel. She used to call them The Plastics – Bramah and Baines. You're talking about people who get on a bus wearing a leather jacket, parking cars with a leather jacket. You only wore a leather when you got on a motorbike. It was a major sin in those days.

I felt sorry for those bikers because they were a pretty good subculture. I used to like them. They had it all worked out – half a pint of mild, half a pint of bitter, a bit of acid . . .

I remember in those days you used to get idiots driving around having had about twenty pints of bitter. Crashing into walls and knocking people over. But if you're on a bike you've got to be very careful about stuff like that. You don't have the protection of the car. I still don't like car drivers. Never learned to drive. I tried to but I can't, don't like it. I can drive an American car, passed my test there. But not here.

Once you've driven a bike every day, like I used to when I worked on the docks – in the rush hour, when Manchester was ten times busier than it is now, when you used to have to drive down the middle of the road – it's hard to adapt. If I get in a van or a car I sit in the back. Still don't trust them. I'll sit in the front seat if it's necessary but I don't like it. I don't like that idea that certain drivers have that just because you've got a car you can go anywhere, with the wind in your hair. It's bollocks. As soon as you buy a car you're on the books. You can't go anywhere without somebody knowing about it.

★

I remember a lot of punk rockers going down to the Monsull estate to The Electric Circus and loads of people from the estate would be hanging around throwing things at them. We were in between. For me it was like CBGBs in New York: rich kids pretending they're trash. And the people round there didn't like it. That's why people like Paul Morley didn't like us, because we'd go up dressed like the people who'd been throwing bricks outside. Not because we were trying to be stylish, but because we were on the dole. All the groups who'd be playing would have sticky-up hair, and their mams and dads would be waiting for them outside.

The only reason we carried on through that was because of the strength of the music, that's how we won people over. I had long greasy hair. I couldn't afford to get it cut – what could you do? I was also very young. The Clash and Elvis Costello were a lot older than me. It was supposed to be people singing about anarchy and all that, but they didn't actually know what they were talking about, they were all public schoolboys – that's what I thought.

To me, punk was a safety net for a lot of people, a refuge of sorts from the reality that was 70s Britain. On one side, it was something that the kids could fall into, and out of when it all got a bit too complicated and harsh; and for the older generation, instead of concentrating their minds on the undeniable mess of the State, it provided them with an almost manageable problem.

That whole scene has been wildly misrepresented over the years; once the revisionists get their hands on something it's hard to seek out the reality. The best thing about it was that it didn't rely on perfection; you didn't have to be a well-schooled musician to be a punk. But, as with many scenes, it became very conservative – with everybody dressing the same and avoiding those that didn't. Small wonder that they soon ran out of things to say.

Even The Clash – who, I must admit, were very good when

they started out, much better than The Pistols – lost it spectacularly. After that first album there's really nothing there; and in a
way, like a lot of those punk bands who wanted to be 'Punk' –
not like us – they turned their backs on their real selves, embrac-
ing all the old rock postures and themes instead of keeping to
what they did best.

That's why I've never aligned myself to the whole punk
thing. To me, punk is and was a quick statement. That's why
most of the main players couldn't handle the fall-out of it all,
they were like a bunch of shell-shocked army majors stuck in
time, endlessly repeating their once-successful war cries. Nothing wrong with that, I suppose, but I wanted something with a
bit more longevity. When you're dealing in slogans like The
Clash and The Pistols it's hard to keep that shit fresh. I sensed
that at the time. It's like when we played live it was – attack!
People at the back of the room would be like – whoa, what the
fuck is this? Quite confrontational in a way . . . But the songs
were more like short stories; unlike every fucker else we didn't
just bark out wild generalizations. Simple fact: we weren't a
punk band. That wasn't my intention.

Hardly surprising that nobody liked us. We played all sorts of
places; used to get a better reception in youth clubs – kids clubs.
You go to a punk club in Middlesbrough and there'd be twenty
strapping guys with their hair all stuck up – weekend punks, we
used to call them – spitting at you all the time. The only place
that would put us on was Eric's in Liverpool. They understood
us. But we always thought on a different level from the punks.
I didn't want to be part of a scene, never have. And I knew it
wasn't going to last. Things like that are very temporary. I think
it had to do with the fact that you have to work at The Fall;
we're not always an easy option.

A lot of the time I was being portrayed as a fool who still
believed in punk. I wasn't at all. Journalists like Ian Penman at
the *NME*, they were all going into avant-garde punk, Scritti

Politti and electro and all that shit. And it didn't really concern me. A lot of that punk stuff was heavy metal to me. We'd been through the pubs and clubs by then. I liked The Sex Pistols; but except for the lyrics they were only the same as the Sabbath and Zep-like bands we were playing with. It was the same sort of music. Not bad when it's good. Sabbath and Zeppelin, they weren't bad.

Look at The Buzzcocks, they went the opposite way – dead pop, which was a good idea as well. Girly pop. We played a lot of shows with them, kept us going.

We'd go on before them and do our shit, some of it was up, some of it down, some of it all in one chord. The Buzzcocks would go on, do their poppy set. Then The Heartbreakers would come on and do a rock and roll drug-addicts set. It was great! And The Worst would come on . . . each had their sound. It stuck out. If you didn't like it you could fuck off. Not like now; it's a dirge now. You don't get that variety. Now all the bands have the same attitude, the chords are not going anywhere. I'm not a musician but I know that, as a layman, that's my advantage – that shit's not going anywhere but downhill. It's depressing to me. It might work for a nineteen-year-old student but I don't think it works in general.

To be honest though, it wasn't a happy time.

I've never been matey with musicians, even then. I think that's where I got off on the wrong foot. I'd had enough of gangs at school. That's where they get upset. Musicians don't like it if I spend time with other people, non-musicians. Who wants to hang around with the group all the time anyway? – you spend enough time with them on the road, for fuck's sake. It's a nightmare to me. I don't think in the same way as they do. It's as if I'm speaking the same language as them, but for some reason or other we're not having a conversation.

I remember The Buzzcocks, not Pete Shelley, but the rest of them, saying that we'd be a good band if only you'd get rid of the lead singer. And the band were taking notice of this, I know they were.

They didn't want to be in The Fall. The whole concept of The Fall back then was mine. They didn't get it; members of the audience did, but not them.

So, in their own way, they were already against me. They didn't think I had it in me. They'll say different now, but that's a fact. It's still the same: people waiting for me to fall on my arse and fuck up.

Always makes me laugh with former members, they all want to be together, but when you get down with them and are together they don't like it. You want to walk around with me all the time, you want to follow me around, then I'll come out with you – it's like the group in Arizona – Ben, Steve and Spencer. If you want to follow me around I'll come out with you, then they start going, 'Oh, I don't want you to come out with us.' Then of course I'll say, 'Well, I am coming out with you. I will go to the sound-check. I will sit down with you. I will talk about all your problems.' And of course they don't like that. So what are they talking about?

They like to complain. But if anybody really complains, they don't like it. There's no backup for it. I've sat down with loads of musicians, and said, what's the fucking problem, and they go, nowt! Or they start talking about money. Well, I'll give you the money. And still that's not enough. They want the best of both worlds, they want to sit down with loads of people, but they're not willing to commit themselves properly. They think they're superior to people in gangs, people in the street – it's always the same. What are you going to do?

Voices 1

I hear the grinding of knives. I confuse the hosts by moving on. They're eaten out. I have no time other than this. I don't sedate as easily as they . . . Dresdenized . . . A city ravaged . . . A carcass left kicked. Loosed the demons . . . Everything rained on . . . He thinks he's more man than the rest. King Dick. And she's the sort of bird who'd look through the dictionary for the meaning of the word psychiatrist . . . 'You're like this weird mix of Adolf Hitler and Gandhi' . . . 'Just call me Andi' . . . They're unable to mourn the passing of their youth . . . The lyrics are often cut up and difficult to understand . . . Constant Experimentation . . . Many a time he's exploded . . . They reek of self-pity and confusion . . . I'll meet you in The Red at 3.00 . . . I'll meet you in The Woodthorpe . . . Drink . . . I hope to become an afternoon amnesiac . . . The dead remain piled: mouths agape . . . The hanging room in The Ostrich. Don't go in there. There's a reason why it's always empty. Nobody goes in there. Well, only those that don't know . . . These bad instants. The unhinged . . . Bald stalker's back. Boozer's skin . . . Those flats over there; great times. I'm getting fucking sick of the fucking builders next door; from seven till seven. Salford mate of mine said he'd go round . . . They don't know what

time they're living in. They're in rewind . . . I'm having it
he got pushed . . . You can't be a hard man with a soft
heart. If you two weren't here I would have kicked the
fuck out of him . . . Ten years ago I would have followed
him to the train station and kicked the fuck out of him . . .
They're not your real mates, though, are they? They say
they are. That's what they say, anyway. But you're not
telling me that they're your fucking mates . . . Any man
fond of throwing a kazoo – that most proletarian of
instruments – into the mix . . . I'm on the hard road
again. And if you're not in the exhibition – go boil a
chicken . . . He came round at about twelve with a bag
of cans. I was a bit fucked by then. But he started singing
that . . . In a drunken sleep, I dreamt of soft drinks . . .
They keep sending me letters about sorting my bins out.
Bury Council. Blue bin for that. Green bin for that.
Brown bin . . . Piles of Holsten in the same bin . . . I'll
wait up for them. Stupid cunts. Stupid Bury accent . . .
I'll wait up for them and yell obscenely . . . An accepted
inaccuracy and inarticulacy is the common tongue . . .
Pounced on by midges . . . There's never been a way into
people . . . She was never all there . . . I got on the bus
the other day and there was this bald bloke who kept
staring. I've seen him around . . . He wears powerful
blandness . . . Spitting lyrics like coughballs . . . You get
judged so much it doesn't matter any more. Let them think
what they want. I'll throw them a v-necked v-sign for their

trouble . . . 'I lost 65,000 words of my self-help book and I need to get them back' . . . And on the plane back the air-conditioning . . . I don't know why I acted like that. The band was okay. The visas were sorted. I don't know. It's weird. It's not the first time. You just get worked up . . . He poured water all over Steve's suitcase. I don't know how he got in there. And he's trying to put a cig out on Spen. Spen just banged the door on him. Nearly broke his arm. Told him to sober up . . . I looked at him and I knew he wasn't up for it . . . Perpetually frightened of nameless threats . . . Different fucking matter when we're talking unpaid chokey debts. They think they're ruleless . . . Rock and roll became more serious and less important . . . Demmicks . . . Her circus of the face . . . This old mate of mine used to look like Peter O'Toole. He was great. He'd take ages to get ready. You'd be waiting for him downstairs. He looked good though . . . I remember being in The Church on acid. It's like a Hammer Horror pub. Everybody turns round as you walk in. Log fire. It's that sort of mentality . . . They're all fucking coppers and mouth-almightys in there anyway . . . There's always some mad cunt on the fringes. I don't know what goes on inside his head . . . Ringing up, threatening people. They don't think I know. They think it's all alright and I'll just fucking not say a word and let them act like fucking . . . We'll have a change of scenery today. Meet me in The Old Monkey . . . I don't know where you're going with this . . . Why are we

still talking about Rough Trade . . . Is it not finished? It
should be finished by now, surely. If it's not finished in
three weeks then I'm canning the fucking thing . . . Nervous breakdowns. Young lads losing it . . . You alright for
money? I know what it's like . . . It's never easy. Will that
do you? I'll post it through the letterbox . . . Can you do
me a favour and put the typewriter in the office . . . Put
some pictures of me up on the wall . . . It's the same as
always . . . I've known people to just fucking lose it like
that. He came at me. This big cunt . . . I think he's a
sleeper. His dad was a communist. How did they afford
to fund him through university? His mum was only a
cleaner. It's because of his dad, that's why. That's how
. . . Watch him when he comes out of those meetings with
all the other leaders. Grinning. They put something in his
food years ago . . . So-called member of the sane society.
Bollocks. They're the worst we've had for ages . . . You
wouldn't even get that shit in Cuba . . . I think they had
the right idea in Russia. You can't go round talking like
that. Not with the likes of them. I'm having it more than
him have been poisoned like that. I bet the restaurant's
pissed off . . . They were going to bomb Old Trafford . . .
Foiled . . . Incurably ineffective . . . He prowls the stage.
A brooding presence . . . When will they get new words
. . . Backs against the wall. Piss-head. Speed . . . Cig in
face. Cig on arm . . . I could give up smoking today. Now.
But I don't want to. I like them. I like the taste.

And what's with that Man United fan? His mush, his big red mush contorted with the animated delivery of constant speak, like a gargoyle lurching out from a horror-film mansion. Shooting me a look; maybe he knows; maybe he works the night as well . . .

5. The Group/s and their Useless Lives

I find it hard to talk enthusiastically about the ex-band members thing. I don't understand the big deal with it. They came, they saw, they fucked off and now I no longer see them. I find it all very boring, to be honest.

The Fall are about the present, and that's it. The reason I'm quizzed about this so much is a combination of general, unenlightened curiosity by people who are amazed that it keeps happening and why I'm such a bastard for letting it happen; and because I'm not in the public glare. That's what fucks them off. That's why those other books don't work. It's like that bloke from the *Guardian* who nearly had a nervous breakdown saying, 'I can't get to the point of you.' I said, 'Well, look, you're only supposed to be interviewing me for the new LP.' I'm telling him it has nothing to do with me. And Simon Ford with his book, *Hip Priest*; tracking down the ex-members . . .

There's something there that they don't like or don't under-stand – what's the point? I think you've got to make a stand against this attitude that everybody's life is common knowledge; when it isn't.

I remember when *Through the Keyhole* was the only outlet for all this heightened prying. David Frost and Loyd Grossman – they're the culprits. And Madonna. She was the first to orches-trate people's idle interests, to make the private a public free-for-all. And now she wants her privacy back. That's the sort of people we're talking about here. I, on the other hand, have never bought into all that. I find it grotesque that people spend their time in such a way. Imagine looking back on your death-bed and remembering the days you spent reading up on these air-wasters. You can switch on the internet and find out what Beyoncé had for breakfast. You don't actually find out about the lyrics of these people, their ideas, etc. What's it for? Who's it for?

Let's get it straight here – this is not a book about them. The Fall is about more than just disgruntled ex-members.

You can read all that shit everywhere else.

I'll only talk about the following for the benefit of the ghost-writer and the publishers . . .

Karl Burns (drummer – signed in 1977/sold in 1998)

I met Karl Burns in the old Labour Club headquarters in Prestwich above what is now the great and wonderful Bargain Booze. I'd go down there with my Irish mates. Sit around and discuss issues in a self-important way, like those old do-gooders Marx and Engels. Actually, the main reason for turning up was that you could get a late drink there, but you had to be a member. And, as with most things, and especially where drink is involved, it helped if you showed a little bit of willing.

At the time, Karl was the drummer in a group with Vini Reilly out of Durutti Column – it was like Vini's secret life. He never used to play clubs; but on the sly he and his band would play all the hits from The Who and The Stones and The Beatles in pubs. I got talking to Karl. He then came to the first gig and said to us afterwards that he could do better . . . And it just worked from there. He was a very original drummer. He was better than anybody around at that time; everybody else was shit in comparison to him. He was an original and that's what we needed.

We had a bit of a love–hate relationship. He could be very nice but he could also be a bit of a bully – he's a big fellow, but

I was one of only a few who could control him, who could stick with him.

After a bit, I got fed up with policing him. He'd show you up with girls in dressing rooms. I was very puritanical at that time – I didn't like having girls backstage. I'm still a bit like that. The groupie world – you don't need it; it causes a lot of problems. That's how we usually fell out: he'd get a girlfriend and his work would go to shit. I'd say to him, 'You're twenty-odd, why are you acting like a fifteen-year-old?' He'd disappear on tours and come back a week later. Meet a bird and fuck off. Good job we had two drummers. I wasn't having that. With him it was third time unlucky when the sparks flew in America. He was getting really bad at that time. He didn't have the fire any more.

You've got to keep fit if you're a drummer. It's alright for me but not for everybody else. You start lying to yourself if you go too far. Stop believing in the right things. The worse thing is that it gets harder to cope with the doubt; once you lose the belief, then you're surplus.

I'm not saying I know what I'm doing all the time. I don't. But I do believe in what I'm doing; that's the difference. It's a lifetime thing, and he started talking himself out of it long before he bailed out on me in New York.

In the end he became his own audience. He wasn't sure of his role.

I've not seen him since The Ark broke up, and I don't miss him . . .

Best drummer we've had is Orpheo – one third of The Dudes. He's got a lot of different styles that integrate into soul stuff but don't intrude. It's not that obvious. There's a bit of Caribbean in there every now and again; but he doesn't know it himself. I like musicians like that. Karl sedated his creativity in the end. I couldn't be doing with that.

Steve Hanley (bass – signed in 1979/sold in 1998)

First time I met Steve Hanley was at Eric's in Liverpool. Just before *Dragnet*. I remember watching him and thinking we've picked the wrong bass player in Marc Riley; because Hanley and Riley worked as roadies for us once every two months or so, and it was clear Hanley was the better of the two.

He was in this Christian band called Staff 9 who used to do all these old Christian numbers; just before U2. We gave them a support at Eric's for a laugh. So we got him in and switched Riley to guitar.

He was always very loyal. Always gave a good performance, good at organizing things. I think he just got fed up. The finances were going up and down at the time – one day we'd all be on good money and then six months later we'd be booted off a label or I'd leave a label. I think it was the uncertainty of it all. Like many, he found it hard to live like that; pressure tells with some more than others. Eventually he said, 'I can't really cope any more.' But this was before he bloody dumped me.

I think the quiet ones are usually the worst.

Craig Scanlon (guitar – signed in 1979/sold in 1995)

Craig Scanlon was always very good, to be honest. Looking back, it was a big mistake getting rid of him. He was a bit of a sacrificial lamb. The group was getting a little too big and nobody was actually doing anything and neither was he. He may have just burnt himself out. But I must admit I wasn't at my best in the mid 90s either.

I looked on him as a co-composer. He was another original, but like a lot of those guitarist types they want the credit but not the responsibility. They want a say in all the songs but they don't want to fill in the tax forms. And when the going gets good, they start acting like Keith Richards. It's a syndrome. But it's not very Fall. I've found it with a lot of guitarists.

I think I've been too slack sometimes. It's my job to keep the band fresh. I'm always looking out for the musician's benefit. If they've got to go, then that's it. The benefit of being in a group is it's not like being in a standard job. It's not fixed. You don't have to return home with a pissed-off mush because you've heard enough from the cunt sat next to you.

You shouldn't be in the position where you start hating what you do. You can see that this is the case with a lot of people, but they stick at it. The worse thing about that is you can hear that the zip's gone from their game. It's the Beckham syndrome again. People always let you down. It's a truism. Not only that but they let themselves down as well. The only thing you can do about it is write about it.

I suppose I have pissed a few people off with my way of doing things. People accuse me of being arrogant or self-centred or just plain ruthless when it comes to relationships, working relationships. It's as if I'm the only one who's ever thought of themselves as at the centre of this blue and green ball. Suddenly they're all innocent and sinless. It's ridiculous. You're not telling me that nobody else has ever thought the same way. It's barmy. They can't handle that I'm willing to admit it and that I don't hide it; because they're the fucking same in a craftier way.

We're talking about adults here who have the right to choose. What the critics and ex-members don't realize is that I can call on just as many other people who'll tell you a completely different tale.

I'd be dead if I just acted the way they say.

The post-Fall life really gets to a lot of them. It's as if they've been to Vietnam or had a particularly fraught space-excursion and their senses have been obliterated. That's all they can talk about, that's all that remains in their fried heads. I'm thinking about setting up a post-Fall-syndrome therapy hour. That'd chase a few wolves from the door.

If I was to go round and apologize for everything I've ever done I wouldn't have any days left in me. And The Fall would be non-existent. And whose version of the truth rings loudest? It's hard to get at. You only remember what you want to remember.

The way I see it, there've been a lot of good bands who have worked hard, but in the end they didn't know when they were at their best. The Fall, on the other hand, have lots of moments when they are at their best and this is because of the constant changes – this is what counts in the end.

The detractors might say there's never really been a Fall – that there's been too many members, that I've just pulled the wool over people's eyes by running it like an unhappy guest-house. I'm immune to all that. You can see how thin their lives must be when they start talking like that. There's no point getting worked up about it, largely because these people haven't got a clue about music. Show me the rule book on how 'things should be' and I'll concede defeat; until then . . .

I say to everybody who enquires about this side of The Fall – do you still work with the same people you worked with ten years ago? That's how I look at it. That's the way I am. People are shocked by it.

To me these ex-Fall people are just anybody in the street now. I'm not really into asking them how they are and what they're up to now. It's not bitterness or anything. I'm like that with ex-girlfriends. I find it weird that couples hang around with each other's exes; how they're all still mates and they all go out together. They can't cut it off. I'd never ring my ex-girlfriends up. There's no point in it. You see it with a lot of musicians – they still hang around with each other even though they split up years ago and can't stand each other. Split up acrimoniously even. You can see they don't like each other. They're still bitching about each other.

I only get ex-members back if it's a real emergency. But it always backfires. It's useful for a bit, and then whatever parted you in the first place surfaces again. It always does.

Interlude
The Two-Year Gap

It's always in my head, with everything in my life. For instance, I'm working with a musician but we're going nowhere – I think he's good, he thinks I'm good, but it's not happening. So he has a fit, or I have a fit. And we split up. This is what the ex-members thing is all about. I'm not interested in them. But the two-year gap is really a truce. Two years later they'll come to me and say, you were right all along and I didn't realize it at the time. But you can't keep waiting for these people. That sounds condescending – but it is a two-year gap. I get people coming up to me asking where Brix is – I don't fucking know! I don't care. That's what keeps me going. They've got their priorities all wrong. People don't like being told the truth, though. In 1997 I said they were dicks for voting Labour – but nobody was having it at the time. Three years later people are saying – 'Oh, you were right there, Mark.' It's a waste of time, really, but I still do it. Nobody likes the bringer of bad news. What makes me laugh, the older I get the more people repeat things that I told them ten years ago. But whereas five years ago I would have had a rant at them – 'I fucking told you that in 1997!' – now I just go, 'Oh really, that's interesting.'

Some people aren't as fast as other people. Some people have different talents. I can't use a computer. I still use a pen and paper to write.

6. The Fool, The Magician, The High Priestess, The Empress, The Emperor, The Hierophant, The Lovers, The Chariot, Strength, The Hermit, The Wheel of Fortune, Justice, The Hanged Man, Death, Temperance, The Devil, The Tower, The Star, The Moon, The Sun, Judgement, The World and Eric the Ferret

You don't know what you're in for with The Fall.

I mean, you couldn't have a Mark Smith school of writing lyrics; hopefully not, anyway. There are times I've wished I could knock out hits. But I can't. There's a skill to it, and it's not in me. It's no use trying, really.

I always try to write a Eurovision every two years, but there's no way it's going to happen. Most records I bring out, I just think this is what it should be, so it's irrelevant what other people think.

And I don't worry about writer's block. I've never had any real problems – a couple of weeks, maybe, without anything, but nothing serious. Something will always fall out of a bag for me. I'll be waiting for a line and it'll come out of the bottom of a bag with a receipt – I'm a very lucky man in that way.

I usually find that the more you try, the less it works. It's best not to force it. When people do force it you can always hear it. It's just not how it should be. What gets me is the lack of lyrical effort shown by bands nowadays. I'm not saying that everything should be literary and Dylan-like: thirty verses of fifteen-syllable words that even the band get bored of playing. Me and Elena use that thing on the telly with the subtitles to read some of the lyrics. Jesus Christ! 'I'm going up the hill, you're going to leave me, I'm going to leave you, why did you leave me?' It's pathetic: all meek and self-absorbed. I'm just not interested in hearing about some lad's break-up with some college girl he thought was the love of his life and now he's had a few too many and can't remember who the fuck he is.

Lads today are a bit too open like this anyway: going to the doctor's every five minutes telling them how depressed and distanced they feel. And they're not really depressed, not clinically – it's not even disillusionment. It's something else, something that they've conferred upon themselves. I think it's because they've got too much time and space to think about themselves. You don't get lads like that in Russia. It's not part of the culture there. It's a uniform, if you ask me: an identity. You can hear the whingeing in their music. It's stale. They should stop hiding away in their bedrooms with their computers and get out a bit. That'll sort out the lyrics.

All my songs have got lives of their own. Otherwise they're not worth doing. I've thrown lots of stuff away, though. I've always got a book of writing on the go, and I get it out of the bag when I'm doing an LP. Mostly it's just shit which I thought was good at the time – stuff like 'Jeremy Paxman is a monster' – well, maybe not that bad, but phrases I've put down when I've been up at night.

You've got to edit yourself. I'll go through a few pages and find a line that's lovely. That's a really good feeling.

The number of times I've lost lyrics is amazing. Sometimes I've left them in a pub in an Aldi bag . . . A funny thing happened when I was in America with Tim, Rob and Orpheo. We were driving through a desert, carrying around a bag of lyrics for the new album, *Reformation Post-TLC*, and we stopped off at a petrol station in the middle of nowhere. I opened the door to get out, to stretch my legs, and this wind just blew the bag of lyrics out of the door. There were sheets blowing everywhere.

So I'm trying to chase after the fucking things. Then this little lad appears from nowhere and picks them all up. And I'm like, 'Cheers, cocker.' Things would have been much different but for him, the little man in the desert.

I find it good if I'm under a bit of pressure. If the bass player's moaning about his taxi money, and asking what we're doing next, and you just hand him a sheet and say – that's what we're doing, on the spot like that, more often than not it'll work. 'Insult Song' on *Reformation* was done in one take. I was just fucking around – the tune was there and I just started ranting, making things up. But it worked, and in a way it's the story of that period when the band fucked off and left us in the desert. And the new band loved it as well – I was just using it as an exercise, but they wanted me to keep it on there.

What surprises me most is how much of my stuff doesn't date. I often think when I'm recording it that a particular song will, but it doesn't date as much as you think. 'Sparta F.C.', for instance, is a weird one. I remember thinking, that'll go over their heads, or under their heads. But it didn't. And 'Bingo-Master's Break-Out!', our first EP – it was very weird at the time to write something out of tune like that. But it still resonates.

In those days everyone went on about how I couldn't sing. It's a very British attitude. I can actually sing if I want to, and I could then. But the thing is, if people are saying you can't sing, you end up shouting the lyrics out as hard as possible: when in doubt, shout. I still do it now. That's what soul singers do. Otis Redding – he's not *Pop Idol*, is he? He just belted it out.

Songs like 'Industrial Estate' – that was the second or third song that I wrote the music for, but the lyrics came first – it's a sort of poem; a hard poem. You can tell it was written at work. It's about working on the docks, on a container base. So of course I presented it to the group and they want to know what it's all about. They would prefer me to write about velvet shiny leather, the moon and all that kind of thing, like Television or The Velvets. As a compromise I wrote the chorus – 'Yeah, yeah, industrial estate' – to make it a bit more American rocky. And I wrote this sub-Stooges music to go with it, Stooges without the third chord. At the time, people thought it was terrible because it wasn't the way it should be, it wasn't 'in tune'. But I never wanted The Fall to be like one of those groups. I didn't care what people thought.

That's what grabbed me about The Stooges. You can't imagine how hard it was to get hold of Stooges LPs in those days. I'd harass every record shop in town when I was nineteen to get The Stooges. I'd keep going in every week, take a day off work, post off for it – anything. I used to get all this shit from Virgin Records: 'No, we haven't got any Stooges LPs but why don't you try this, *Tubular Bells*, it's on special offer.' But it was worth it when I got it. There was nothing like The Stooges in the 70s. They weren't hippy–drippy. I'm not a guitarist, but I can play their songs – I like that. That's what's great about them. And the fact that they wrote the first album in a night is fantastic. They only knew about three chords and had to get it down. Not enough bands work like that nowadays. They're too precious. It's The Stone Roses syndrome: five years to record an album. Just get in there and fucking do it! That's your job.

You can work at things too much, do too many takes, make it too clear. Strip it of its mystery. When we recorded the first album I had a sore throat, but the studio time was booked. So the bottom line was we had to go in there and record; no fucking around.

People misinterpreted that album. They thought it was too serious, overlooking the humour of it all. That's the story of my life, actually. People can't quite get it, so instead of giving it a bit of time and sticking with it, or even just not bothering with it, they'll talk a load of crap about it. People like Paul Morley. Paul Morley never liked us, and now all of a sudden he's written an article in the *Observer* proclaiming The Fall as the best thing to come out of Manchester. I think he's earning money off me. That's my attitude. I don't want to live in their world. And neither do Fall fans.

Every time I get a good review in the *Observer* or the *Guardian* I get worried. And when Paul Morley starts saying nice things about me I get more worried. Status Quo used to say that the day you're on the front cover of the *NME*, that's the time you start worrying – I agree with them.

People forget what it was like. At the time we never had any money. When Kay Carroll got involved in the late 70s she was just a working-class housewife who'd got divorced. She had nothing else to do. She knew what she was talking about. She knew what it was like to work in an office and have the boss feeling her arse every day when she's got two kids at home. She was well into it, managing the band.

We were one up on a lot of other people – John Cooper Clarke, for instance, was a beat poet and The Buzzcocks were music students – but me and Kay had actually worked. It's all right saying, 'You'll all be on the same wage,' as they did at Factory Records, but that was the deal when I was on the docks. I might as well have gone back there, earning a wage. We wanted the money for a fair day's work. We wouldn't play for nothing. We still don't. It's not an extension of your art-school course, it's work.

Unlike a lot of bands who just wanted to play in each other's back gardens, we were willing to go anywhere. We did a lot of working men's clubs in the north, a comedian's audience basically. Les Dawson wrote a very good book about that scene: *A Clown Too Many* it's called. I never liked his comedy, but that book's worth looking out for. They didn't like us in the Midlands, though. They wanted everyone to be like Led Zeppelin, not a bunch of kids in jumpers.

I wouldn't go back to those days, but in a strange sort of way it was fairer. Now the promoters are all drama graduates and media graduates telling you how late you are. Whereas the owners of those places would just say, 'Get on, play loud and do it! You've got a hundred people in here!'

Most of the time, the audience weren't bothered about what you said and did. Half of them might have hated us because they'd just come out for a pint and a plate of chicken and chips. But in a funny sort of way they tolerated you. And a lot of our core fan-base originates from that period, and from those places. People who didn't like rock groups. People who did just go out to see comedians. They're still there now – the Yorkshire Fall Army. God bless 'em.

John Cooper Clarke was a big help as well. He used to live near me in Prestwich. I've always got time for him.

We couldn't get anywhere to rehearse in Manchester around 1979. You had to be on the Factory label or a lardy-dah band . . . it was all The Nosebleeds, The Smirks, The Buzzcocks. We couldn't rehearse anywhere. At least Tony Wilson was honest about it in that BBC documentary – they didn't like us in south Manchester at all. But Clarke let us rehearse at his house in Salford. It was tiny. He was great, bringing us cups of tea. The neighbours would be complaining and he'd be telling them to bugger off. All his mates would come round. He was always very encouraging. He gave us a bass player – Eric the Ferret. He was useless, but he meant well.

Clarke doesn't go on about it, even now. He was just into what we were doing. At that time he was doing stuff with Martin Hannett. I liked the lyrics but I thought the production was horrible.

He was very laid back. I'd say to him, 'Look, Clarke, I can't afford to pay Eric the Ferret to drive us to London,' and he'd say, 'It's alright, Mark, have a joint – I've just got a big advance off so-and-so,' – whatever label he was on at the time. 'You can still borrow Eric – useless as he is.' That's proper behaviour.

For the first two years we weren't bothered, we didn't want to sign to a major. I had Richard Branson ringing me up at the end of '77, asking me if I wanted a deal, and I just said, 'No!' Two years later, when you finally get your first record out, you might regret that – but I don't really regret it. It was the right decision. Who wants to be one of the thousand Virgin groups to have been dumped over the last ten years?

I used to earn money playing pool: me and Kay – doubles. Pool tables were a new thing in pubs at the time. Beforehand it was all snooker tables. As a result, few people had got the hang of it.

Me and Kay would take teams of brickies on, Irish labourers – they'd look at me and look at her, and go, 'Yeah, we'll have a bit of this.' About eight of them. Making these remarks to me . . . So we'd let them win a couple of times, then thrash them, and walk out with fifty quid each, all their wages – it paid for the rehearsal place. We needed the money to finance the group. I would never dream of ringing my dad up and asking for it.

I used to do tarot readings as well. I went through a phase of reading books on the occult. I was fascinated by it. I still believe that things leave vibrations. America, for instance; I've visited all these old Civil War sites and the atmosphere is incredible. You can almost reach out and feel it.

Bramah used to do readings as well. But after a bit, when the drugs prevailed, it got ridiculous. I got more interested in the Philip K. Dick *Time out of Joint* angle – the way certain pieces of writing have a power all to themselves, almost as if they can prophesize things. But I still did the readings. Kay had a lot of hippy mates, housewives with a bit of money, really, who were always seeking out people to read for them. And I had a natural talent for it. I've always been able to read people. My mam's a bit like that. I never used to charge a lot, but now you can earn a fortune. When I was really skint in 2000, I thought to myself I should be doing that again. You could earn £40 an hour.

When people did a tarot with me they'd walk away with their life changed. But you can't fuck around with those things too much. You're dealing with a force. When it goes wrong you're not being a vessel. You start getting into what you think the person wants to hear, what you think they should be told. But if you actually just let it go, with strangers especially, you find it's usually exactly right. I got quite a reputation for it. It's very draining, though. Poker and other card games are a bastardized version of tarot. If you keep losing at poker or cards, then you're a loser, there's no two ways of looking at it. But in a tarot you can suss things out, and put them on the right track, whereas in poker you've just lost a million quid there, pal. Poker plays on people's vanity and greed, it's a very down experience. To me, the difference between tarot and card games and poker is like the difference between reading a book and watching a film and TV. Tarot is a book, cards is like watching a film and poker's TV – a now experience. Tarot's a much richer experience. You get what you want out of it. Nobody really loses with tarot, unlike poker, where you can come out depressed, like watching TV.

I did the readings for a year or two. But people started coming back too much. I had to tell them to stop. You get to the point where people can't function without it – once a week turns into twice a week. They were driving up in their sports cars outside the flat, asking if they should go with this nice man they'd just met. A lot of fellas used to take advantage of that. Telling them they need more tarot – and that the tarot says you need sex with me.

One of the rules of the tarot is that you shouldn't really take a lot of money for it, like psychics. It's not good. So I'd take presents, a nice leather jacket. You'd go round to dope dealers and they'd give you two ounces of dope per reading. All their readings would be like, 'You need more advice,' i.e. I'll come back next week when I've run out. Especially if you're rich.

I've got that type of face that people want advice off – I get it all the time. It must be the nose or the way I drink.

Voices 2

Talk about long days . . . Sleepless for days . . . Stare
at the *Mail*. Borrowed town. Eat shortbread. Radio 2.
Regress. Open can . . . I stand in the full light of play. I
feel now. I hear them rewrite the past. They need a
version of truth. Need to forget. Like kids caught . . .
Points a gun. Drunk . . . I'm in a car and it isn't England
. . . Long drives. Talk about long days . . . 'Could you
vacate the car please, sir.' And minutes before I was
talking about Yogi Bear . . . I get back. Light enters the
odd room from dingy angles . . . He stands so much in
the shadow of play . . . Their music is cutting edge . . .
the . . . cutting . . . Spent drinking with men again . . .
Sharp as a cue ball. Past exhumed . . . Blank and autistic.
Some late city. Hotel mornings. Nescafé sachets. A hill
of pillows. Retired shower . . . You can hear your hair
grow out here . . . I'm having it he had it planned all
along . . . Mark without the M . . . I hear the city breathe.
And blood sneezes . . . A mass of phlegm that's been
balling the wall of his mouth. Dropped on ash. In The
Red at 7. I'll meet you in The Red at 7 . . . Fancy a nip?
. . . R.E.M. wail. From station café . . . My train is now
pulling in. It's a comeback album . . . There's a thread
that runs throughout. They never knew what the fuck

they were doing ... Fingers like cigs; as thin as ...
Homeless tan. And the black bull misery ... Angst afternoons. They can't even make it to Birmingham on time
... V for Vendetta ... Worm. Guilt ... The absence of
scruples. The crime of aggressive war ... My house is
smaller now I'm older ... Marks and Spencer's doesn't
want the likes of us in there ... What's wrong with you?
They're our people ... Telling me he's from Edinburgh.
Drinking like a rock star ... Why don't you go home and
type it up instead of acting like a rock star? ... Sloppy
cunt. Why you sitting like me? ... That's the word he
kept using ... Sloppy ... American radio ... Cowswitchz
... I knew it was the wrong idea to get the plane. I
should have stayed. Reckon you can get me back on
tour? They spew shite. Walking unreal pantomime ...
Snakes in San Francisco. The lung association. Keep tabs
on tabs. Too busy feeding fucking snakes ... German
snuff ... Some sort of music dripped from the speakers
... Brix smoothed out the edges; brought in a snappier
look ... Did she fuck ... The McGyver effect. Breaking.
Things. Down ... Pop. 1280 ... How to influence people
and talk dirty ... That's what they want to hear. Influ-
ences ... Nothing in their own heads. They all want to
be me. *Guardian* vendetta. They eat loneliness. All willing
to bare their insides to fill a night. Full of piss and wind.
Clever negativity ... Town flesh ... Hotel bedroom. Ants
below window. Smart as whips. Sunshine unkind ...

Ignorance in action frights . . . For turning up here's a Holsten. I'm more than a can of Holsten . . . Ill omens of the permanent underclass. Twenty-five now and all your ideas gone. Fucked . . . He looked nervous in the interview. She's a slag. Lazy journalism. They're all the same . . . Empty logic becomes you after time. I've not seen Karl since . . . the Hanley brothers . . . The Fall army. I should have a word with The Fall army . . . The perfect hour. Brought low . . . Rigsby pilled up. No. 6 . . . You would have loved it. Loads of birds for you to look at. Nice rider for you to drink from. Sun . . . I release them from the pains of the normal working environment . . . He meets the world . . . Impotent Labour. And Elvis . . . Head music with energy. The Manchester Music Collective . . . Arndale CCTV . . . Bury market. Saturday. Busy . . . About the present and always will be . . . At the ICA, The Mall . . . How years turn and dip. Without equal. More or less equal. No pictures of me . . . I've got traps on my door. Nobody in there . . . Scary fuckers don't scare me . . . The community feel of American radio . . . The music sounds jagged. Franz Ferdinand fans will not know what's hit . . . Whistle and I'll come to you . . . Drink; that blessed curse. Feels like a slow kill . . . 'Worst film I've ever seen. Nothing fucking happens. What was it called? *Lost in Translation*? I wish it was . . .' Ground control to Gene Hunt. Decades unkillable . . . Hellfire. Let's have it like Man in Black . . . Thin like cigs . . . We'll have one in The Old Monkey.

Celebrate ... Not enough smokers on TV. Not like Russell Harty ... Have you been locked away somewhere? Distance dictates this thing ... Mind if I shoot ... Just like flies. Don't write too many good lines. They pilfer. Them ... Black rooms in the Roosevelt. Bowie walls ... Crystal methskin ... 'Yeah, did you not know? It's made from cleaning products.' Pure gunk ... The downhill struggle of ... Bono. Branson. Frankie Machine. I can't write in the present. Out of the woodwork. Out of the dust. They'll be back soon. And they'll think it's going to my head. Changed ... I am writing this at 23.46 so all may not be as it should be ... They never used to let you in without a gun. Let it be said. I am not one to shirk mirth ... The applauseless life ... More kids at the gigs now ... I am in constant repeat. He always sounds the same. Drings like a srunk ...

And the door opens and the cold enters before him, whispers his name.
And he sits down and slips me the package wrapped in an Asda bag:
another mobile, the fourth in four days.

I put it on the floor, near to my feet, within eyeshot, and ask:

'Pint?'

But he's out the door. Gone . . .

7. They Who Dare!

I've never really got on with record companies. Knowing how they operate or mis-operate, it amazes me how most of them manage to keep afloat. To be fair to them, Step Forward were good to us in the beginning. They seemed to be into the same thing. Miles Copeland was financing it – the record industry didn't like him because he was a millionaire's son, but he gave us a chance, because he heard something different in it, like he gave The Police a chance. The fact that he was Stuart's brother is by the by. The Police were laughed at as well, because they were doing pop reggae.

You had the freedom there. We were treated very well. There was never any pressure. When we did *Dragnet* in 1979, it was a new group, totally different music. Step Forward heard it, thought it was good, thought it was rock and roll, thought it fucked up the mainstream. You have to remember that Miles had a background in Wishbone Ash and Curved Air – he was sick of it, really. He'd done all that Spinal Tap-type shit before. We were out of this world for him. *Dragnet* was so opposite to *Witch Trials* – which I think is still a powerful LP. But *Dragnet* is the other side: the horror of the normal. I like that sort of stuff; with writers like M. R. James and Arthur Machen the stories are right there on your doorstep. I used to be in the Machen Society. I started reading him when I was about sixteen. He's one of the best horror writers ever. M. R. James is good, but Machen's fucking brilliant. He wrote a great drug story, *The Novel of the White Powder*. This is way before Crowley and all the other commercial occultists. His stuff's quite terrifying. You can see where the likes of Robert Bloch and Stephen King got their ideas from, using the mundane everyday as a backdrop for great terror.

The Machen Society was brilliant, you'd get these fantastic excerpts from his unpublished diaries – a good film could be made out of them. He lives in this alternative world: the real occult's not in Egypt, but in the pubs of the East End and the stinking boats of the Thames – on your doorstep, basically. I know what he means.

I always imagine his stories being read aloud in a fruity academic accent in a study in an Oxford or Cambridge college in winter, with the mist rising from the river, the only light coming from candles, and the only heat from a large fire and the bodies of the small audience. He was a great writer.

I'm a dreamy sort of person and I get on with this sort of writing much more than I do with realists. I never wanted to be bracketed with the realists – *Dragnet* has nothing to do with the reality of the times.

We recorded it in three days. Most of it is purposefully out of tune. But later we found out that Cargo Studios in Rochdale didn't want to let it out. It was a heavy metal studio and they were nervous about releasing it because of its sound. They thought it'd reflect badly on them. But Step Forward were great. Miles and journalist Danny Baker, who was a rare fan of ours at the time, were saying, 'Just bring it out – it's The Fall!'

They were different times then. Even though it was the arse-end of punk, it wasn't the done thing for a studio to release something that sounded so wilfully alien to everything else. In their minds this meant sabotaging future projects with the likes of fucking Marillion.

It was quite strange listening to it. Even the band were unsure about it; but I loved it. It's funny, because it was the first album that Grant Showbiz produced. I'd met him at the Deeply Vale Festival in Rochdale the year before. He was there with a load of hippies, living in a bus with no clothes on, no joke. He's forgotten all that now. Then I got him mixing for us and mixing for The Smiths and now he's like, 'Oh, you know what Mark's like after too much whisky!' and 'Oh, I've got to go and work with Billy [Bragg] and I've got to go and work with Mozzer.' I remember when you were in a camper van in Deeply Vale mud, Grant! He didn't know what year it was!

Grant's very London. Everywhere to him is London. He's done some good work with us over the years, so I shouldn't have a go at him. But once certain people start supping with *artists* they tend to forget the origins of this new existence; and in truth, he didn't know what he was doing on *Dragnet*. It panned out okay, though, and looking back it wasn't such a bad thing using an inexperienced producer. We were much more willing to take risks. We worked it out as we went along – but not in a half-arsed way. It helps, sometimes, not to be too precious about these things; on occasion it'll throw up an idea that was never there in the first place.

I don't know why people found the album so objection-able. With the journalists, I think it was a simple case of them expecting one thing, having written the copy for that one thing, and then getting something else and thinking, 'Fuck! I've now got to think about this.' It's hard for a lot of journalists to get to grips with a band that keeps moving. They try to pretend otherwise – that all bands should experiment more and not play ball with the industry so much. You hear it all the time. But whenever this happens, their writing falters, they can't seem to erase that notion they had of the band. It requires too much effort. Whenever we get a good review, it reads like a good review from 1986 or whenever – 'And Mark Smith is back with another LP of rockabilly and penetrative lyrics blardy-blah . . .' I've read it all before – they've read it all before, they're copying themselves. It's as if we're too far ahead for them to truly understand what The Fall are about. Good bands need a good audience too. If you don't come across as readily as, say, U2, who are defined by the amount of records they sell, then journalists struggle to write anything perceptive about you. They don't allow themselves the time. If you're not a comfort blanket or a doom-monger then what are you in the eyes of journalists, who only seem to have two or three angles to write from? They don't read enough, if you ask me. Writers should read, and I know for a fact that all too many of them don't – they get their qualifications, fuck off travelling for a bit, return to London, get a job in the media and don't bother to put any more ideas inside their heads other than the two or three they picked up at university. I'm not talking about striving to be an intellectual – they don't even have any historical perspective on anything. It's one long Friday night to them. Or if not that, then you sit down with journalists or so-called far-out types in London and they'll be saying, 'Oh yes, you won't believe the way the wife breastfeeds!' and I'm thinking, 'Alright – good for you!' They have fuck-all interesting to say for themselves.

The worst thing is, they get employed very easily. It's no wonder the media lacks depth – one idiot is enough but twenty-odd of them are bound to fuck things up. I find it strange that these sorts of people have a go at Fall fans. Writing about how they're all the same – ageing blokes wearing wind-cheaters and all that, supping pints of bitter: moaners, basically. What's the difference between the fan and the journalist? Both have their viewpoints on the way things should be. I don't get it; I don't think there's anything wrong with the opinionated fan who does a job in the week and then for one night has a few beers and goes to watch a band – what's wrong with that? Why not write about that angle? You're bound to have a group of nostalgia-men in the house; even Oasis have fans like that. It's more about the journalist, about their life, than the subject they're writing about.

The only thing I do find annoying with Fall fans is their tendency to reminisce too much about the early days. I find it hard to look back at things like everybody else. They seem to have different eyes from me, fondly reminiscing about Karl Burns, about the original line-up, the purity of punk, about events like Deeply Vale. Deeply Vale was fucking heavy, I remember that. It was in its third year and by then there were about twenty-odd thousand people there; and no coppers. All these morons come to beat the hippies up, all these big Rochdale fellows with enormous heads. Some of the biggest people I've ever seen live in Rochdale. I don't know what it is. The blokes are huge. I've recorded there a few times over the years – we finished *Reformation Post-TLC* there, at Lisa Stansfield's studio. The Dudes came over from America – Tim, Rob and Orpheo. I remember sitting in a pub with Orpheo and all these lumpen Rochdale blokes are in there with dents in their bald skulls, belting down pints. He handled it well, even though they were just staring at him every time he opened his mouth. He was too un-Rochdale for them. They didn't *know* him. I think he wants to move there now . . .

I can't look back like some fans can. I can't get beyond the fact that most of it was shit – most of the people telling me otherwise are daft cunts like Paul Morley and all those other talking heads who make money out of that sort of shit. It's blatant revisionism, if you ask me. Programmes about how great the 70s and 80s were – it's always the same people peddling the same story – don't they have anything else to talk about? Thing is, if they weren't making that sort of programme then half of those idiots would have to go and write about something proper. Odd thing is, they don't even talk about the few good things that originated from the past. You look at a programme like *The Prisoner* – now, do you really think the people pushing those nostalgia lies have the talent or patience to create something like that? A single episode of that or *The Twilight Zone* has more ideas in it than a full year of modern TV. The difference is that back then they actually cared about what they were doing –

that, and the fact a lot of the writers working on those programmes had a background in literature. It was proper writing:
original writing that tried to work on different levels. It makes
me laugh what they get away with nowadays. They just don't
explore the medium that they're at the centre of, they're frightened. It's not just TV either – music as well. When we recorded
those early albums we never thought about how the record
company would react; not like they do today. I wanted to write
out of the song – 'Spectre vs. Rector', for instance. I wanted to
explore, to put a twist on the normal. People think of themselves
too much as one person – they don't know what to do with the
other people that enter their heads. Instead of going with it,
gambling on an idea or a feeling, they check themselves and
play it safe or consult their old university buddies. That's why
it's all so staid. They've only got about four ideas between them.

The late 70 and early 80s were a strange time being in a band.
I quite liked the way that everything was a little fragmented. It
meant that I could get on with things and the band not moan
about which other band they thought we should be sounding
like. I remember when we released *Totale's Turns* in 1980.
Nobody wanted to release it, because nobody played the sort of
venues that you hear on it – places like Doncaster and Preston.
It wasn't the done thing to promote ourselves like that. The
north was out of bounds; it might as well have been another
country. But I know a lot of people who rate that album; it
reminds them of The Stooges live LP – *Metallic K.O.*

It didn't help that I was in my early twenties at the time. It's
not acceptable to be headstrong at that age. A lot of people are
still like that in the music business. They don't like people who
know what they want, at the best of times; but they like you
even less if you're sticking to your guns and you're under the
age of forty. The thing is, I don't deliberate like most other
people. I know when something's done, when it's time to work
on something new. It rankles with musicians. It's amazing how

many of them just don't know when to stop. They think it's a marathon; a marathon of perfection.

With *Totale's Turns* we just pieced a load of tapes together. They were lying around in a studio somewhere. In the band's eyes it was commercial suicide releasing this dirge; they couldn't see the soul that lay behind it. That's musicians for you.

The interesting thing about being in a band is that a lot of people who want to get up and go on stage are quite reserved in normal circumstances; but part of them needs to be seen. So they join a band with another three or four people with the same unspoken problem. But inside there's a lot of bile. In a way they resent the man at the front. You only have to look at Oasis. I've never really liked Noel Gallagher. Liam's alright, I like him. I feel sorry for him actually – it's always our kid this and our kid that, always his fault. I'd hate to have a brother like Noel. What's he doing? Liam is Oasis – he's handsome, he's a good front man, great voice. What does Noel do except write Beatles-type tunes? I've met him a couple of times and you feel like saying, 'Shut up!' I think he's a bit jealous of Liam – very Catholic, that. Liam's done a lot more for them than he's been credited for.

I remember meeting Noel in America in the late 90s. He went to the bathroom in my hotel and I had all my shirts in there. I could see him through the mirrors looking at them, seeing what brand they were.

A mate of mine called Hubert told me a funny story about him. He came to Prestwich once, in the early days of Oasis, pulled up in a car with one of his sycophants and asked Hubert where James's recording studio was – James the band, 'Sit Down' and all that shite. Hubert hadn't a clue who he was. He wouldn't have been bothered anyway. But he said Noel was very impolite, asking for this studio. So Hubert asked him if he was a Fall fan. Noel said he wasn't. Hubert's like, 'You go down here and then you take a left; and then another left; and then you go down there . . .' Not a clue where he's fucking sending him. Serves him right.

That whole pre-*Grotesque* period was a phenomenal learning curve. It's horrible how much people try to shape what you do. At the time I was very sensitive about this; I still am, but I don't beat myself up about it as much. I had a lot more untapped anger back then. And hearing other people's silly verdicts on what I did just made me worse.

I wrote about what was around me; that was the whole point – to get down the experiences, scenes, people, etc. But some people are so daft they don't understand that writing about Prestwich is just as valid as Dante writing about his inferno.

There's nothing stranger than the things you know but don't quite realize. Pointing it out is the difficult thing. But you can bet that once they get it the world has changed in a weird little way; it's an altered state. But it works the other way as well. And it happens in a flash. It empties you a lot more than you think. I've been lucky in that respect. But I've known people who've returned from London after a week or two, or even just a night, and their entire creative mind-state has altered beyond recognition. All at once they're rootless. The London body-swap has skinned them. I see it also with people who have gone and 'travelled'. They lose so much of who they are they can't retrieve it, they just float around talking about travelling all the time. No stories or anecdotes, just talk of more travel, of more time in Cambodia or somewhere else equally as fucking impoverished and war-torn. It's a similar mindset to that of ghoulish celebrities who quietly travel out to Congo with a school of cameramen and journalists. And once they get there they can't wait to start picking up young kids with half an arm. I find that very odd: celebrity healers.

Imagine being a young lad or girl from outside London and then you're thrust into the London record industry. Imagine the peer pressure that goes with all the partying. Most record companies, most major record companies that is, hire enough staff to cover hangovers and the rest – the emotional breakdowns and whathavya. It's the new wilderness: the moneyed wilderness. These big companies have all this covered. As soon as you start partying too much, start turning up for work with webbed eyes and a mouth like gravel, like the fast-money kids did in New York in the late 80s, you're out of the door, and the day after another one enters. Then where do you go? I've seen it loads of times. A good friend of mine used to write for a men's magazine, one of those crap lifestyle magazines. Every month he'd have to review a car or a cricket bat or something. But after a few years of it he didn't have it in him any more – the bullshit had got to him. But instead of kidding himself and hanging in for the wage packet and the nights out, he wrote a letter to the magazine, exposing it for the sham that it was. And then fucked off.

He's never worked since.

He had just returned from interviewing Hunter S. Thompson, though. Maybe the fact that Hunter had taken him out for a drive around Woody Creek at six in the morning on acid might have had something to do with it. Things might have seemed a bit skew-whiff after that!

People underestimate what places can do to you. If you're not a space cadet you're alright, but if you walk into these things blinkered then beware the vampires. I've been avoiding them all my life. The fuckers are everywhere.

I left home young; not like lads nowadays, who live at home until they're thirty and spend all their money on cars and hair products and bad ecstasy. I never had big dreams about travelling. I know a lot of kids who did; who got homesick for places they'd never seen. Even when I did romanticize in my music, it was always about Manchester, because that's what I knew best.

It's similar to when the Victorian writers would romanticize about places like the Orient. They'd never seen it. It was just one of those places that fixes itself in people's heads, like Australia now. And when they eventually made it there, after slaving enough kids into the ground, they discovered it was awful.

It's even worse nowadays. Kids start saving up to go to Australia when they're about seven, harbouring notions of the *Neighbours* life before they can even chew their food properly. It's time to eradicate this idea that by getting away you'll find yourself or walk into a glorious new existence. People who think like that just want rid of themselves. Where you're living is in your head.

I know the address he wants it delivered to. I've seen the lights on at night in those long, long windows; seen the cars outside, the teenage bones scattered liberally along the gravel path.

But for the stories I'd sleep; but there's something in the stories. I can't escape the stories . . .

No more lithe lads with shorn skulls peddling small bags of low-grade bugle. No more girls with tikka masala tans totalled on White Lightning and the giddy rush of new love. No more young; their history ripped. Gone . . .

8. The Year of the Rats

1980 was a bad year . . .

New decades tend to make people fragile and more unsure than they've ever been, but 1980 seemed to be particularly barmy.

The problem started soon after *Totale's Turns*, when I began thinking of albums more in the way of documents; elongated newspapers, so to speak. 'Fiery Jack' was a turning point; I guess in hindsight you could look at it as the beginning of *Grotesque*.

I've always written from different perspectives, but that one seemed to have more weight to it. I still see 'Fiery Jack' types like that. They're quite heartening in a way. Manchester has always had men like that, hard livers with hard livers; faces like unmade beds.

Even though they're clearly doing themselves damage, there's a zest for life there. And that's a rarity. They're not as oblivious as you might think. They're not all boring cunts. Drinkers have a good sense of the absurd. I like that.

What pissed people off with the stuff from that period – *Slates* and *Grotesque* – was the position it was coming from. But I knew what I was talking about. I wasn't just dropping in for a couple of afternoons to observe the beer-minded proles. I was more than just a can of Holsten. And, what made it even worse, I was on to Step Forward. It had swiftly turned into a bum deal, and you weren't supposed to speak out about stuff like that, especially being a northerner. You were seen as a whistleblower. Basically, their idea of distribution wasn't the same as ours. I'd go to record shops in Manchester, looking for a copy of *Witch Trials* or *Dragnet*, and find nothing. There's no point recording if it's not in the shops. It's not enough that you're just on a label. You might as well do it all yourself if that's the case.

In retrospect it's alright *Mojo* magazine voting *Grotesque* the best Rough Trade album. But at the time it was bloody murder. You think to yourself you've got it bad now . . . But instead of the two-year gap it's the twenty-year gap.

I was never certain about Rough Trade. They reminded me of kids at school who suddenly get into things. I remember being into Bowie's *Man Who Sold the World* when I was a kid; all the other lads at school were listening to fucking Pink Floyd. Bowie was off the radar for half of them. Six months later they've all got fox-coloured hair and they're all acting fey and spacey. Rough Trade were like that, but in a business way. It was as if they'd returned home from school, yapping about this new thing – indie music – and their mam had given them a few quid to go and immerse themselves in it – to shut them up. But they're nowhere near as radical as they think. That's why we buggered off from them as well, after *Slates* – that was the final straw. They didn't want to bring it out because it was a 10-inch; neither an album nor a single. I wanted to release something that could be bought by the working man. Too much stuff released around that period seemed to overlook this particular corner of life. The likes of Geoff Travis at Rough Trade and his ilk; they were only arsed about entertaining their mates round the corner.

And sure enough, they didn't like the sentiments behind some of the records. People forget: 'Slates, Slags etc.', the actual song, was totally un-PC for Rough Trade. They didn't like the phrase 'male slags'. A lot of so-called hipsters are very conservative like that. There are more taboos in their world than there are in that of the fucking Tories they purport to despise.

On top of that, they'd always have people interfering, people who were supposed to be working on the cover. I've got no problem with quality input, with genuine ideas; what I can't abide is those who just stick their hooters in for the hell of it, because they're at odds with their jobs. They wanted lyrics to all the songs and stuff like that – it was like living in Russia. I was living my own Cold War.

'Well, Morrissey gives us a lyric sheet.' And of course he's into all these causes – women's lib and gay lib; not to knock him – 'And "Slates, slags etc." doesn't quite fit in with our label,' and all this tosh – 'And what exactly is a Prole Art Threat?' It was a very arty-farty time – all Aztec Camera, Scritti Politti and The Smiths. They were supposed to be against the Duran Duran types, but they were just the same in my book: poseurs with acoustic guitars instead. You get bands like that nowadays, nothing changes. I'd had enough by this stage. The strangest thing about it was that it'd come out after *Grotesque*. It wasn't as if we'd hit them with that straight away. You could sort of understand it if that was the case. But they knew who the fuck we were.

The initial beauty of Rough Trade was in the contract – fifty to them, fifty to the group, which was very innovative at the time. But I just ripped it up in front of them. I never actually signed the contract. Nobody owned our output. They wanted a more commercial, 'Totally Wired' style record and I handed them *Grotesque* . . . Everybody was giving me shit, journalists saying people don't want to hear songs with a story, where are the messages and why aren't you addressing the political climate, etc., etc. Stuff like 'Container Drivers' and 'Pay Your Rates' was very unusual in those days. Groups didn't record rockabilly country and western songs about these subjects. I even had problems with the group as well, they didn't like it, couldn't get their heads around it. They wanted to be The Jam. But in my eyes *Grotesque* was the first record that worked as a whole. And like always, it was me fronting it. I refused to bend.

I loathed all that Gang of Four sixth-form political stuff. Still do. I always thought we were a lot more mature. Even when I was younger I was never into decadence and teenage angst – The Gang of Four were a form of that, if you ask me. I wanted to appeal to intelligent listeners. This is why we kept politics at arm's length. We'd done all that Rock Against Racism shit in the 70s.

It all got a bit ludicrous. For some reason a song like 'Container Drivers' wasn't on. I guess because it wasn't a ham-fisted attack on the state of the nation. There's a very interesting book that sums up the pebble-dash thinking behind berks like that – *No Retreat* it's called, by these two ex-soccer hooligans, Dave Hann and Steve Tilzey, who went from being hooligans to going out and wapping the National Front. They'd hunt them down and bottle the cunts: the correct way to deal with them. They used to steward for the Rock Against Racism lot, but after a bit they got rid of them, said they were no better than the violent NF. Booted out by the people they were fighting for! It's a very English mentality.

We were dealing with a generation of guilty people, who had taken all the drugs in the 60s, had a few kids in the 70s and realized that they were exactly like their parents after all. It's a very middle-class thing, rebelling against your parents. Most of the people I know who are working class like their parents because they know what they've done for them. But then of course these people aren't in positions of authority, not in the main, anyway. But it seemed to me that a select few people were hiding behind this idea of false concern in a really half-arsed and sentimental way.

We'd done a load of free gigs for RAR, and then The Clash and Tom Robinson came on the scene, and all these other pop groups, and all at once they didn't want to know The Fall any more. The minute Polystyrene, or whatever her name was, and The Clash said they'd start doing them – which they didn't used to do in the 70s – things changed irrevocably. It became a Bob Geldof type of scene – they wanted the most famous people to get the message across. It didn't bother me. I've never needed to attach myself to anything, and I'm deeply suspicious of people who do. Geldof's a brilliant chancer. He's built a whole career on Live Aid and do-gooding; a whole career that wasn't there before. I mean, who listens to The Boomtown Rats and who buys his albums? At least Bono, for all his faults, has a career outside of all that hand-shaking.

Joe Strummer was no different. It was terrible the way he died, but it needs saying that he wasn't the savviest cultural commentator. His politics were all over the place; bluster over substance, that's what he represented. We supported The Clash in New York in 1981. Belting out naive generalizations in front of this backdrop that went from the Yorkshire Ripper to pictures of kids being coshed; all very clichéd. It was like watching the news in your living room with The Clash playing in the corner. Everybody knows it's wrong. But coming at it from that angle is pointless, thoughtless even.

The sad thing about it all is he distanced himself from his middle-class background and education, appropriated this tough heart-on-the-sleeve messenger stance so convincingly, but lacked the wit to take it anywhere fresh. He was preaching to the converted, and I don't just mean his fans, but himself as well. He daren't offend anybody, because they'd just charge him with being a phoney, and he daren't look at it in a sceptical way, because then he'd be employing his privileged education. That was the crux of his problem.

Anybody who came up to me in America asking about the British music scene, I'd just tell them it was dire – stick to what you know, stick to driving music. Don't get me wrong, I've always been proud of where I'm from. I'm just not into that musical imperialism that so many bands suffer from. You need a bit of it, but when you start crusading into America with that sort of attitude you just end up looking potty. They're not as vapid as you think, Americans. They concocted their entire history from lies, so they're not going to buy into some limey's glorified head-trip.

Grotesque is a very English album. It's written from the inside, from experience; the real thing. Pub men can tell you a lot about the English way. But it's tricky, because it wasn't a defence either. It wasn't some sort of kitchen-sink apology; or even one of those crap salt-of-the-earth things, where the working class are delighted with their lot, trudging around potless and pissed.

I don't really write from a solid idea. It's never that certain at the start. You get to what you're saying through the writing, the process; and then you move on.

But the place for *Grotesque* certainly wasn't indie music.

Even though it wasn't respected at the time, it won us a groundswell of support. That was the great thing about it. People of a certain age, say twenty-five and upwards, said that it was their record, they related to it – not people in groups who heard it as nothing more than a naff LP recorded by a bunch of pony musicians, and certainly not the critics. But the most telling aspect of that period was the fact that I realized there's a lot of ambitious people in this country without the talent. It's a disease.

Factory wanted to sign us after this, but I wasn't going for it. That's what Tony Wilson's gripe was with me. Rob Gretton, who was one of many partners at Factory, used to say to me that you all had to dress the same, same trousers, have the same haircut, wear the same sullen expression and you all got paid the same. So Joy Division got paid the same as The Stockholm Monsters and so on.

Rob was cool. Every time I met him he used to say he admired me for not signing. 'That's the biggest mistake you ever made,' he'd say, in a jokey way – because Joy Division got big. 'The amount of groups that come round here creeping, arse-licking to Tony . . .' I was at arm's length with it all – thank God. Rob used to lend us equipment and vans, but he'd always say, 'Don't tell anybody. I'm only doing it for you because you're a City fan.'

The question with Factory is – where did all the money go?

It was a factory system. You had to do what you were told. It was based around the Situationists: cultural terrorism, subverting capitalism and public spaces. Good in theory, but it's a bit different when a south Mancunian like Wilson is at the helm. In my view it wasn't that far removed from the original factory days. Engels was a factory owner in Manchester, he had twelve-year-old girls working for him, probably in the same buildings where the Hacienda was. A middle-class socialist; same as you've got now. He'd observe the kids and write about how depressed they were. Who does that remind you of? – Tony Wilson! He went on about how these working-class kids like The Happy Mondays were drug addicts; interesting degenerates. I think he knew what he was doing talking like that, because when it all went tits up they heaped the blame on The Happy Mondays.

The problem they had was when they started hiring people who clearly weren't cut out for that line of work; mates of mates and whathavya. That never works.

But those people are very powerful – those media graduates. Maybe not as much with the Factory lot, because you could keep an eye on them, they weren't holed up in London. But they can make sure you don't work again. Labels like Rough Trade and all that – even now. It's an unsaid thing. Rough Trade's revitalized now; must be in their craw that we're back as well.

You do sometimes get the impression that these labels are deliberately trying to destroy you. In a way, Factory tried to obstruct us when they signed The Happy Mondays, because they wanted a Fall and they didn't have a Fall. That's probably half the truth. I'm not having a go at Shaun Ryder and Bez – they're alright. I've always had a lot of time for Bez, in fact. When we won the Mojo award a couple of years ago both

Ryder and Bez presented us with it. It was a funny night, that. Bez was still wearing his outfit from this car programme he was presenting – this jump suit with a load of pockets on it. He was walking round asking U2 and all that lot for drugs – hilarious. You can't take the scally out of Bez. I remember throwing things at The Gang of Four – beer mats and whatnot. And Bill Wyman and U2 were asking for more free wine. Cheapskates.

The power these labels have is quite frightening. The connections they've got. We've never taken big advances – not then and not now. We're autonomous. All these independent labels are the worst. People are just realizing it. Major labels aren't right for The Fall all the time, but at least you know where you are. The independents pay you less, they interfere and they're all in each other's pockets.

If you're on a major you get 20 per cent of a record and if you're on an indie you get 14 per cent. The other 6 per cent goes to indie guys who drive around pretending to be indie. That's the bottom line.

In a strange way I think Factory were content that it ended like it did, when it did. Mancunians are not very good at handling success. They're more into instant nostalgia, knocking out a few records, making a slight impression then going underground. They're the enemies of longevity. If you look hard enough beneath the pavements you'll see them with their flares and spliffs talking about Wednesday nights in the Hacienda.

It's the polar opposite of the Yank mentality. I think that's why Mancunians are so well liked over there. They probably see it all as a brave artistic retreat.

But the worst thing is that the city hasn't recovered from that period. What with that and the gentrification of the place . . .

Before the bomb in '96 Manchester city centre was populated by some of the best Victorian architecture in the world. You could read history off some of those buildings. They were masterpieces – beautiful combinations of science and art. It's not like now; it's just a bad Rotterdam now. Toy Town. I don't know what it is with architects. Buildings nowadays are not symbols of progress; they're the result of too many minds regressing into childhood. Just look at them – glorified toys built grand. It's as if they've just stubbornly excluded the trusted expertise of the older lot because they're new to the game and it's their duty to change things. They remind me of those fellows who thought they'd redesign the docks in the 70s; and look how much they achieved. Nowadays, the ultimate aim is to force the working class out, that's what gentrification is all about. They think that by building glorified fridge boxes and passing them off as 'modern' and 'progressive', everybody who walks by will in time transform into the likes of them!

Degrees have a way of warping people – it's not good for people to spend that amount of time at university, acting like rock stars on weekdays. They get so distanced from the real world they haven't a fucking clue what's needed. It's a luxurious prison, almost. Once they get out, once they're released, they're good for nothing other than having weekly reunions with their old housemates, getting jobs with their old housemates, or staying on to receive more educational therapy or forming piss-poor bands. And they've all got floppy fringes. They all wish it was 1980 and Joy Division were still around. Uniform mentality: my aim is to steer well clear of anything slightly resembling that.

We did a European tour on the same circuit as the Rough Trade groups, the likes of Stiff Little Fingers. Nobody had a clue what we were on about. It was very strange. We had a conga player instead of a drummer, this insurance salesman guy, because the drummer was too young to play over there. We would play to stony silence doing the *Grotesque* numbers.

Everybody would either be a Factory type or a pub-band type, or in Germany it'd be a load of Kraftwerk types. It was all rather disheartening.

The prevailing idea was that you had to be a punk or Bowie-ish, and we were neither. It's no wonder you start appearing negative or cynical in interviews; dealing with dead-legs like that doesn't make for good relations. Simply put, nobody wanted us there. And you can take it personally and start picking at yourself or you can just keep trucking on. The overriding factor of it all – back then and even now – is that too many people are devoid of any humour. And if they do have a laugh, it's in the vein of business humour – a forced, Christmas-party idea of a good time.

But I knew it was right to hang in there and stay true to The Fall. The important thing was being hit by the simple fact that there are no rules when you're writing. I'd always thought I was ahead of the pack anyway, but I expanded at a phenomenal rate at this point. The earlier stuff was a little hemmed in – it didn't look out as much. When you're hit by the knowledge you can write about anything, if you've got the imagination, that's a powerful feeling. Nothing's wasted; you think you're idling hours away, but a lot of it comes back, a lot of submerged thoughts and ideas. When you finally realize it, it's obvious, it's less of a struggle.

I think this is why I ended 1981 stronger than any other year. I saw no point in shying away from these cunts; that's what they expected. That's always been my way. Even now, I'll ring record companies before the postman's even got his trousers on. Hit them when they least expect it, when they're barely awake.

Looking back, you can see how MTV profited from these people. It was only a year later they started brainwashing kids and record companies. It all boils down to an easy fix – strait-jacket your acts, get them to deliver simple sentiments, simple albums, and all of a sudden music's no longer something you carry around in your head but just another piece of TV. I understand that it's always been about money; that's a given. But there's something inhuman about the way in which it's put into practice. And the swiftness of it all! From idealistic punks to moneyed indie chappies. I prefer to stay away from it all; attack them from the comfort of my abode with a nice cup of tea and The Chuckle Brothers on the box.

9. Silence of the Riley

We never depended on John Peel for our livelihood. I don't put my career down to him.

I had an argument with Marc Riley about this on a train. We were shouting at each other, like some daft couple. He was saying, we've done two John Peel sessions and isn't it great. And I'm saying, 'So what? It's only the BBC. We're not a fucking rock band.'

The idea was that you did John Peel, then progressed on to the 7 till 9 slot and so on. We never went that far from Peel, and ultimately that was a limitation for us. You become known as a 'Peel group'.

I warned Riley – if you think we work for the BBC we don't, we work for who we want to work with. He thought we were like Peel's party band; that he could call on us any time and we'd be straight down there to play for him.

I had this idea that Peel was a starting point to better things, like the morning show. It was a process.

Anyway, when we brought out *Hex Enduction Hour* Peel dropped us for a year or two – because it was on a random label. He wouldn't even play 'Hip Priest' on a session. It was too long and dull. People look at history though rose-coloured glasses. You've got to remember that to him I was selling out when we covered 'There's a Ghost in My House' and infiltrated the charts. He probably thought I was doing a David Bowie or a Marc Bolan and that I'd never return to being 'Mark' again.

But eventually he got the message – the two-year gap; and he was back into us.

I never saw much of him, to be honest, just a few times here and there. I gave him a copy of Malcolm Allison's autobiography for his birthday; great book that. That's how this book started out – it was just going to be a list of all my favourite drinks and hotels: fuck all to do with music – that would have been funny.

A few of my mates once went out for a drink with Allison, when he was still the City manager. They went to a Chinese restaurant. Allison was dressed all flamboyantly as usual, chomping on a large cigar, ordering bottle after bottle of champagne . . . These mates of mine are thinking, 'He's alright, Malcolm, a good sort, a good laugh.' And then the bill lands on the table. Malcolm picks it up and holds out his hat – these mates of mine throw in a few notes, thinking Allison will sort the rest out, why else would he now be walking over to the head waiter? Two minutes later the waiter comes up to them and says, 'Your friend just told me you'll be paying the bill.' Allison had just fucked off! They were paying for the pleasure of his company.

I liked the fact that Peely wasn't a Manchester United fan – that he supported a decent team like Liverpool. It's a shame that he's not around any more. He was a one-off. I know that his radio show meant a lot to a hell of a lot of people, but I was never a huge fan of it myself. I preferred it in the early 70s. I heard a lot of unusual reggae records through it. But I know people who listened to him religiously.

I can't see him being replaced very quickly. Everybody's too frightened of getting sacked if they play a record that might awake the interest of the listeners. It says a lot when Radio 2 is at the top of the ratings charts. It's like a whole generation of kids are in search of their parents' minds and tastes. Their entire existence seems to be built upon re-enacting their mams' and dads' lives. It's scary.

They're an odd bunch at the BBC. I remember having to meet these two media graduates just before they started filming that documentary – *The Wonderful and Frightening World of Mark E. Smith*. What a pair they were! One of them was this girl, a festival type, a Jo Whiley-ite. She'd just come back from some festival or other, and that was all she could talk about. She hadn't a clue who The Fall were, or who I was. She reminded me of one of those *NME* journalists from the 80s who'd try to get me pissed and fire all these leading questions at me, hoping that I'd react like somebody demented.

First thing she did as she sat down was cross her legs as if she was about to do some fucking yoga – a modern hippy, in other words. I offered to buy her a drink but she's like, 'Oh, I couldn't possibly have another drink. I drank so much at this festival and have you ever been to a festival and oh we saw so many people at this festival . . .' It's no wonder the documentary was ropey. And she never made an effort to get her round in. What are they teaching them at the BBC?

It was the same thing with *The Culture Show*. They interviewed me in Wolverhampton on my fiftieth birthday. Three of them turned up looking like Mork and Mindy and Mork's half-brother. They didn't have an inkling about the band, hadn't even bothered to listen to the new album. They were asking questions like, 'David Bowie's going to be fifty this year but I can't see him celebrating in Wolverhampton on a rainy Monday night. It's very Fall-like, isn't it, celebrating your birthday like this?' I mean, what sort of question is that? For one, I'm not David Bowie – it's a poxy comparison. And the fact that we were playing Wolverhampton was because we were booked in to play Wolverhampton on a Monday night.

You can see why Peely was being shunted all over the place. It's because he was an enthusiast who knew what he was going on about. You're seen as a threat if you display too much knowledge in those circles; or if not a threat then a nerd. It's something that needs to be seriously addressed, in my book.

A strange thing happened to me after Peely died. I appeared on *Newsnight*. When that Esler bloke was asking me questions, I looked as if I'd lost it. I wasn't pissed or anything. It might have panned out better if I was. I couldn't understand what was going on. I had the bloke from The Undertones, Michael Bradley, in one ear and some BBC control-room fellow in the other, and another one asking me these questions. I couldn't even hear myself, that's why I probably appeared mad. I didn't understand what the fuck was going on. But my mam liked it. She apparently said, 'He's always very self-assured, even when he's on TV'!

Just after that we played a gig in Liverpool with Ben and Spencer and Steve. Before I was due on, I went for a pint over the road in this strange and terrible bar populated by frigid-looking arty girls and blokes with really black hair.

I should never have gone in. I'm always doing that; dipping in a pub and then regretting it minutes later when some sexless office fellow comes and sits next to me, asking all kinds of inane questions about 'Bingo-Masters Break-Out!'.

Somebody offered to buy me a drink, some ex-Damned fan or other. I usually say no thanks, because you never know what they're up to. Most of the time they're just being friendly, but you get the odd one and you end up sweating the night out in your own Twilight Zone.

So he brings over this pint of lager, sits down and starts talking about Peel and how sad it is and how The Fall were Peel's favourite band and how he saw me on *Newsnight*, and then the next minute he's being dragged away by this large clown – this woman with her face caked in black and white make-up, wearing all leather, all black leather – it was fucking scary. I finished the pint and fucked off back to the venue, did the gig, and then in the van on the way home everything turned upside down. I must have been tripping or something. I could feel a presence in my body. It must have been some voodoo gunge. I didn't crack on to anybody: just got back home and stuck the TV on. But then it got worse. The TV was racing at me and the room had lost its shape and feel.

I went to bed to sweat it out. It was never-ending. I have a very high tolerance level when it comes to shit like that, but this stuff would have killed the next man. I think it was something to do with the oddball who fed me the pint. He was a browned-off Peel-obsessive who took it upon himself to attack the loon who had besmirched his hero on the goggle box.

Don't get me wrong, I like people from Liverpool. I've never had any problem with them. He just had it all wrong. I'm constantly in battle with people like that.

Marc Riley, for instance. At the time you've just got to let them do it, you've got to let them think that they're right. That is my philosophy: always let them think they're in the right. It benefits me because it shuts them up.

The amazing thing is, they start to believe it.

The problem with Riley was he started questioning all the credits on *Hex* and *Slates* and *Grotesque* and *Totally Wired*. But if it had been left up to him and Craig Scanlon, *Grotesque* and *Hex* would have sounded like mediocre Buzzcocks LPs.

Were they capable of writing something like 'J. Temperance' or 'Hip Priest'? You've got to be joking. Just look at what they've done afterwards. I wrote every note of 'Totally Wired' – bass, guitar – told them everything to play. Just because I can't write it down in chords . . . I wrote 'Hip Priest', but every time *The Silence of the Lambs* is shown on TV, which it's used in, the royalties go six ways. I could have had a mansion by now, but it doesn't bother me. Jim Watts thought he wrote 'Blindness'. We did a cover version of Iggy Pop's 'African Man', but using a different title, and Jim Watts is writing to the publisher telling them what he'd written on it! I'm like, 'Jim, it's an Iggy Pop song. You didn't write it.' Jim Watts did write 'Sparta F.C.' – so I gave him 66 per cent of it. Actually, Elena wrote some lyrics, and I wrote some lyrics and the arrangement.

Everyone in The Fall got paid a decent wage, equal shares for everybody, despite the amount of hours I spent in the studio getting rid of Steve Hanley's mistakes, or Marc Riley's, and Scanlon's too. But you need them, you've got to flatter them a little bit.

I'm forever getting letters from people saying, this compilation's just come out, I'm going to see my lawyer. But they don't have a case. That 'Touch Sensitive' thing, Julia Nagle contested it – every time that car advert shows, she gets two thirds. I wrote the guitar bits, I wrote the riff, but I'd rather let it go – she's got nothing on me. If she wanted to take me to court, I'd say, 'Hello, Julia, so who told you to play this chord – tell the truth, you're in court.' The proof is that the songs are always better and different without them. That's what really winds them up. It's always better.

And why have they got the time to do all this? If they're so talented, why aren't they making good music and raking in the royalties?

The bottom line is, I get a third because I wrote the lyrics. I'm happy with that – they're not. It's not about money, it's about bitterness.

It's the same with McCartney. It's nothing to do with money, he's got enough money. It's just that a lot of people believe that Lennon was the driving force behind The Beatles. I actually think he and Harrison were The Beatles – and Lennon was the real drive. With The Beatles you can always see that McCartney is the goody-goody, which I always thought Riley was in our band. But Marc had to be got rid of. I sacked him on his wedding day! I didn't know he'd just got secretly wed. I said to Kay, 'We've got to ring him, we've got to get rid of him,' because he was getting out of hand: wanting to do 'Totally Wired' twice a night, playing 'Container Drivers' with his cowboy hat on and all that kind of thing. Even Kay was a bottler – she got all nervous on the phone. She's like, 'Marc, I've got something to say to you . . .', not getting to the point. So I said, give me the phone – and he says, 'Mark, how did you find out?' and I go, 'What?'

'I only wanted a private wedding, I got wed today.'

Of course, I thought why didn't you invite me then, you cunt? And I say, 'Congratulations, mate, and by the way you're sacked.'

So you can see why he's a bit scarred.

He was fucking terrible when we went on tour down under in '82.

I thought it'd be good for the group to prove themselves to a whole new audience, and I was at that stage where I'd had enough of Manchester. I'd had enough of the music scene; all that psychedelic shit and white honky monody. I get like that sometimes. I felt like Schopenhauer, the German philosopher who kept to the same strict regime every day. He'd get up at a certain time, walk the same paths, write for the same length of time. When I get in that kind of fix, I bugger off somewhere and return with a brighter outlook.

The tour began at the bottom and it pretty much worked its way further down. Karl Burns missed the first few gigs because he'd lost his passport. A dog with a squint had eaten it and failed to spew it back.

We'd been there a few days, we all had jet-lag, and we were all young. We played a couple of gigs and we started getting some really bad reviews. The Australian press were ramming it to us. Reviews were like, 'Why are we putting up with this Pommy shit?' – this is in their version of the *Sun*. 'They obviously can't play. They tried to play "Totally Wired" – this rubbish punk song from England.' And on the second page there's a list of twenty-five Australian groups who are better than any Pom group. It was like a Gary Bushell review, only worse. Racist rubbish – they wouldn't have had us if we'd had a black member.

Australia's not what it's made out to be. I never liked the place.

I must admit, though, we were shit. We had more fans before we went out there than after we came back.

We went to this stupid heavy metal disco after the first gig – which was awful – and the group all started dancing to Deep Purple. I told them to sit down, have some dignity. I was young at the time, but I know when people are taking the piss. But Riley couldn't see this, couldn't see people laughing at him. Blissfully oblivious, he thinks he's The Beatles in New York. He's dancing around with all these Australian cunts, like Patrick Swayze. And I'm saying, 'Get off the fucking dance floor!' and I'm grabbing hold of him.

There are loads of long-haired heroin addicts laughing at us because we've got short hair.

'Get in the hotel, and stay there till I tell you. You don't need to be dancing to "Smoke on the Water".'

And then he started hitting me, in the middle of this disco. He gave me this black eye. The funniest part of it was that me and Riley had to go on this kids programme the morning after. Riley thinks he's on *Pop Quiz*, or *Tiswas*. But this was Australia. The presenter was vicious, he had a bit of the Enoch Powell about him. Riley thinks this guy's going to tell him he's the new Paul McCartney. Riley says, 'Well, we've played a couple of gigs, and it's going really well, we're looking forward to playing the rest of Australia.'

And this guy just goes, 'Isn't it true, Pommy, that you had a fracas last night?'

I started laughing. And then sure enough it cuts to me with my big black eye.

'And here's the lead singer from Pommy-land. Is it true, then?'

I handled it, though . . .

'Ask Marc.'

I enjoyed that.

Their answer to *Top of the Pops* was hilarious – it's called *Countdown*. It was presented by this gay bloke called Ian 'Molly' Meldrum. He was Australia's answer to Jimmy Saville – but not quite as flamboyant. Iggy Pop featured on it in '79, zipped out of his brains. It's brilliant footage – he doesn't answer the questions properly and he's really edgy, narco-edgy. Tracing his finger down Molly's shirt and saying 'G'day' all the time in this rubbish Aussie accent, and then he goes on stage to mime to 'I'm Bored'. The kids in the audience are terrified of him. It's great. He makes Molly look like a gawp.

Apart from guff like *The Sullivans*, the rest of the TV was Yank stuff and British comedies. The cheeky bastards – having a pop at us for being a bunch of talentless scrawns and all they could come up with was this funeral-type entertainment!

I didn't like the place.

They were right behind us in New Zealand, though. They were brilliant. All the local labels put us up in their houses. They gave us the time to prove ourselves. I respect them for that; they could very easily have just listened to the Aussies and taken it as read that we were little more than a new form of headache.

Even after all this, Riley still didn't get the plot. He was acting like President Johnson, saying he's the spokesman. He and Craig still thought they were Lennon and McCartney – that's why I chose that picture for the front cover of *Fall in a Hole* where he's parading himself like a chief swan to all these imaginary fans at the airport. He was deluded. He's from Sale, with two LPs under his belt. It wasn't exactly The Beatles in America.

There was nobody at the airport – just five guys with long hair saying, 'Get in the van!'

I remember going to my local when we got back. I'd been back a couple of days. People were asking why the fuck I'd gone out there. Nobody could understand it. You've got to remember it was after *Hex* that we went out there. I think people were taking us for granted. I'd heard enough about us being this very *English* group. That sort of talk ties you up. It's hard to vacuum it out of your senses. But my mates were cool about it. It helps to have people like that around you. Proper friends. They're not arsed about The Fall really. I'm not that arsed about what they do. We just have a laugh and get pissed. You can go too far sometimes – with the group and travelling. That's one of the reasons why I've never upped sticks and fucked off to London or wherever. You've got to have a base; and people who'll take you at face value.

Tours are very hard to get out of your head. You're still very much there for weeks afterwards. You have these distinctly vivid dreams about it. I can see how it fucks people up. Your body's all over the place. You get these heightened sensations. After a bit you get used to it, but at the start it's an odd feeling.

I'm not surprised when young bands get flown around the globe and return like zombies. All aged and disgruntled and unenthusiastic.

Personally, I don't mind it now.

But nowadays record companies are more ruthless, especially in America. Rob and Tim were on the road for a full year with their band, Darker My Love. No let up. You're that disposable. If you're not willing to get out there, then they'll just cross you off their roster.

I don't need any assistance with that. I'll do it myself, gladly.

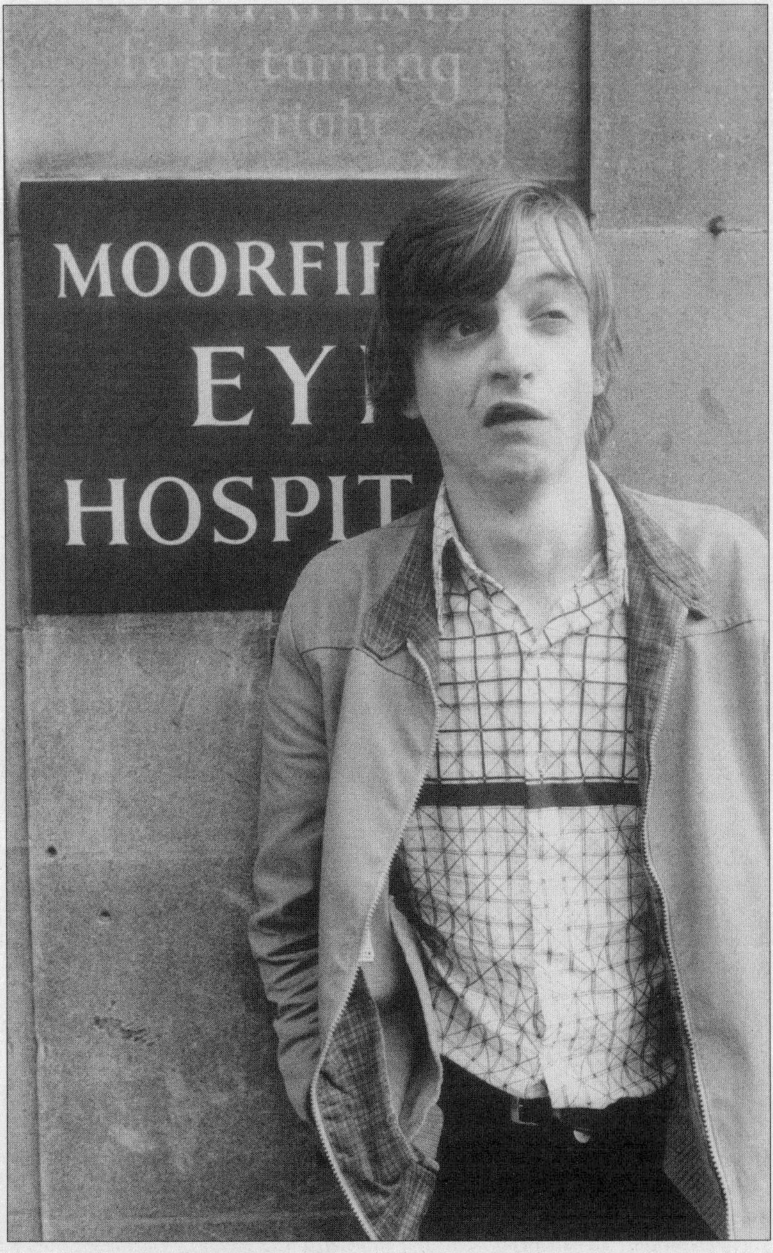
MOORFI
EY
HOSPIT

Lofty told me he'd seen one of them at the petrol station in the small hours. Said it smelled of rank meat, of ancient eggs.

The thought sits in my gut like a broken bottle . . .

10. Operation Cavemen!

Hex Enduction Hour (1982) was a big fuck off to the music industry. It was probably the first time I'd got to a point where I knew I was alone with my ideas. And you can go one of two ways: either you curb your thinking, rein yourself in and buy what they're telling you, or you follow your own path, regardless.

And so I just went for it on that album. But, I must admit, throughout parts of the recording I thought that this is it. This is the last one we're going to do. To a certain extent I always think like that, with every album – even now. But the feeling was a lot more acute with *Hex*. When you're mired in the shit of the times with bland bastards like Elvis Costello and Spandau Ballet, you start to question not only people's tastes but their existences. You're not going anywhere with all that shit. I wanted an album to be like reading a really good book. You have a couple of beers, sit down and immerse yourself. None of those fuckers did that. I don't even think they attempted it. I'd rather listen to the Polish builders clanking away next door than any of that crap.

I'm still very proud of that album. It's the one that everybody talks about, and I can see why. I went through a period when I couldn't listen to it because I thought that I'd never be able to improve upon it. But then I stopped thinking like Costello and realized I had bills to pay and got back on the beat.

I was trying to get the group to play out of time. It's very cyclic this; I tried to do the same thing with *Reformation*: taking musicians out of their comfort zone, getting them to think about timing in a distorted way.

It's weird because I never sing in time. Last thing you want is a regular time. That's the good thing about *Hex* – I was experimenting with speeding up on a track and slowing down. I don't know what was in my head – but I can't think of anybody else doing that sort of stuff. It probably works best on tracks like 'Winter' and 'The Classical'; in fact that song sums up the fuck-you-very-much attitude best. It's the only anthem in there.

We recorded parts of it in Iceland, which was a very inaccessible place at the time, totally unlike what it is now. Beer was against the law. You could only drink shit like pints of peach schnapps. I remember firing into it one day and night. I thought my legs had been stolen afterwards.

The buildings still had swastikas emblazoned across them – they were occupied by the British in the war but they didn't want that, they wanted to be on the German side. That's been covered up.

There was an American base there as well. The Yanks used to practise there because it was the only thing that looked like the moon. But they weren't allowed out of the camp.

It was a great culture, actually – a real Viking culture. But since then it's become just like anywhere else. That happens to me a lot. It's like when you return to the house that you grew up in and it's smaller. The studio where we recorded was fantastic – it was made out of lava. It was like a big igloo. The only people they'd ever had in there were the local poets, who did ten-hour monologues in Icelandic with traditional accompaniment.

We did two gigs, and about a third of the youth population turned up to see us. They'd never had rock groups playing there. I feel guilty for spawning The Sugarcubes and Björk.

We recorded the second half of the album in Hitchin, in an old cinema. There was a great atmosphere in there too. Old cinemas have their own feel like that.

The title had something to do with witchcraft, and 'enduction' I just made up. There's a barrage of ideas going on there. But I don't want to start raking through them. It's a good album, simple. No need to exhume it. I'm pleased with the way Sanctuary re-issued it. They did us proud there. I know for a fact that a lot of kids have got into it as a result. What pissed me off was journalists ringing me up and telling me how brilliant it was, and how ahead of its time it was, and then saying things like, 'Yeah, it sounds much cleaner now.' We're talking about the same journalists who hated it all those years ago. They think I'm so daft, or drunk, that I'll not remember who they are.

At the time though they were all having a pop, saying it just sounds like one long drone, and it's toneless and anti-rockist or whatever stupid phrase was buzzing around the office at that particular time.

I always thought the pure essence of rock and roll was a completely non-musical form of music. Rock and roll is surely not a 'music' form. I hate it when people say, 'Oh, but the production's so bad on it and I can't hear the lyrics properly.' If they want all that then they should listen to classical music or Leonard Cohen – who's nothing but 'poetic'. I'm not about that. Writers like that are too serious and precious about their 'craft' as they call it. There's no fire or danger there, because they've thought all of it out.

I'm not a big music buff, but every song I hear reminds me of some other fucker, and give or take a few tracks here and there you can't say that about The Fall. Something that is original does stand out to me, always has.

The weird thing is that cover versions that are modernized for today's market do work; things like 'Stuck in the Middle with You' by Louise – that's a good cover version. Everything else reminds me of 'Stars on 45' – they were a novelty act from Holland in the early 80s. They'd string all these bits of music together, like The Beatles and Madness and The Buggles. But they'd use the original backing tracks and stretch them so it'd fit in with the beat and the vocals – which is a lot like what they do nowadays. To me it's laughable. I used to piss myself at stuff like that when I was sixteen.

Madonna, for instance – spending two million or however much sampling Abba's 'Gimme, Gimme, Gimme'. What's the point? If you spent a week working at it you could whistle a tune as good as that. It's not just her, though, they're all bone idle. If I was her I'd fling some composer £50,000 to sit in a room for three days and come up with a tune as good as Abba – why not?

I've worked with people like that in Germany, sitting around sampling Can all day. And I'll say to them – why don't you just do something like Can now? Why don't you just write something in tribute?

They get away with it because young kids haven't heard it before. It's shabby. Alvin Stardust trying to be Elvis was cool in my eyes, or Shakin' Stevens even. I thought they were quite funny. It wasn't deadly serious, and they sort of upheld the idea that it was their duty to go out and entertain. It was a thing in itself; not like today, where it's more akin to dot-to-dot drawing. And, in a strange way, they did manage to come up with something new. But you couldn't get away with that today. I always say that about The Kinks: if they tried to get signed up today nobody would have them, no big label anyway, because Dave and Ray's guitars are out of tune and their singing is out of tune as well. And you simply can't have that in today's market.

That's what I liked about Kamera. I have few good words to say about record companies, but they were very good; a world away from the limp stuffiness of Rough Trade. I'm glad I worked with them on *Hex*. I got the right people on that occasion.

It was an old rockers' label. They were heavy metal fans. They'd just say to me, 'Anything you wanna do is alright.' All they were really bothered about was bringing out the best of

Black Sabbath and Deep Purple. They wrote these blank cheques out for us. They thought we were cool because we were working class.

They'd just made a load of dosh from the *Grease* soundtrack album. Old-fashioned rockers – out every night in London. They were all like that Steve Coogan character, Saxondale. He got it spot on there.

They thought we were dead original. Cover? 'Fantastic, Mark!' And it's just me with a felt tip. People forget that a label should support their bands. I used to chop and edit all over the place. But they were always right behind you. And they always hired the best press people – all dolly birds. They had no pretensions at all. You could have just given them a tape of Black Sabbath and they wouldn't have known the difference.

Sadly, they all went insane with Roger Chapman from Family in East Germany. You're talking the Ozzy Osbourne lifestyle here: bake-heads.

I liked those blokes. They're not a bad bunch, the heavy metal lot. They keep themselves to themselves, and enjoy their music. Those old acid-head bikers were like that.

I was very unfamiliar with London at the time, and the bloke who owned the label was always trying to get me out for a drink. A real old-school fucker – he was a good laugh. He took me to Stringfellows. It was great. I was at the bar. There's all these birds walking past us. And George Best is stood next to me. This bloke from the label came and introduced us. Bestie asked me where I was from and what I was doing there. He had about six dolly birds with him and when we were talking he said to them, 'Can you just leave me alone for a bit, I'm just talking to a friend of mine from Manchester.' I thought that was very nice of him.

I told him about being a Blue and how I used to go and watch him with my dad. People did that in those days – one week City; the next week United.

He gave me a lot of good advice really. He said to me, 'Why should I play to 50,000 people a week and get paid fuck all for it? Just get kicked to death.'

I remember seeing him just standing there for eighty minutes on this shabby pitch, holding his sleeves. United were basically playing without him. But then in the last ten minutes he got the ball, dribbled all over the place and scored the equalizer, and just walked off on his own. Nobody even patted him on the back. It's all very well those United players saying how they all liked George. You could see the reality then – they just totally ignored him. They weren't playing with him. He was a different school of football. And I told him that, and he said, 'You're quite right.' It wasn't the drink talking. 'Stick with your game – it's better for you because you've got some control over it,' he told me. It was nice that he took time out for a complete stranger. I can't see Rooney or Lampard doing the same nowadays.

Then I ran into him four or five years later on this programme hosted by Suggs. And he remembered me, strangely enough; he must have been that type of guy. We were on this show, some pilot show, and Suggs is interviewing him, saying, 'You've come off the booze now you've had this implant?'

And he's going, 'Yes, yes, I have,' winking at me.

Suggs says, 'Now we're having a commercial break and when we come back we'll be talking to George about how he's beaten his alcoholism.'

I said to Best, 'That's a bit fucking much – "How George has beaten his alcoholism"!'

So we're taking the piss out of Suggs, and Best says, 'Never mind, Mark,' and from behind the couch he pulls out two bottles of champagne. Suggs is gutted at this, as we're drinking away waiting for the adverts to finish.

End of commercial. 'And now George will talk about how he's beaten the bottle.'

Great bloke, Bestie . . .

I reckon he would have loved it when the Liverpool fans started chanting 'Alky' throughout his one-minute silence at City. That's proper football.

It was a good earner for him, going on programmes and talking about his problems, just the way celebrities do now. I guess he was one of the first to do that. He said to me he earned more from doing all that shit than he did playing football and living in a goldfish bowl.

I understand it. I don't agree with it, but I do understand. Why should he go along and get people spitting at him? People attacking him in the street. Every full back wanted to break his legs. Then he'd come off and get an earful from Bobby Charlton and that piss-head Tommy Docherty. What did they know?

If anybody says to me I've got a problem with the drink, I tell them I do have a problem – like where to get it after eleven o'clock.

I've stopped drinking anyway – stopped half an hour ago.

I find it quite telling that the likes of Bestie and Alex Higgins were castigated in the way they were. The English are jealous of mavericks. You only have to look at Maradona. He's a national hero in Argentina, but not in a sentimental way, like with Bestie – always harking back to what he once was. They love him as he is now, today.

What do people mean by 'lifestyle' anyway? It's a ridiculous phrase. Half of them can't even look at themselves in the mirror in the morning, and they haven't an inch of the talent those fellows had.

I remember meeting Alex Higgins at Maine Road in the mid 80s – he used to practise up the road from me at Riley's snooker hall. I think he still does now and again. Apparently it's very nice there.

It was a David Bowie concert – the Spider Tour or something, boring as fuck. Tears for Fears were there – I was sat behind them.

Higgins said to me in the bar, 'I'll talk to you later – I'm going to go and see how the match is going on. Very nice to meet you.'

Thinking it's match day!

He walks out of the room and there's all these VIPs there and Tears for Fears are sat on the end, and he clocks into them, fucking falls into the little curly-haired one as 'Space Oddity' is playing. And he carries on falling down the stairs, fell flat on his stomach. I thought it was hilarious.

I like the snooker guys. Higgins and Jimmy White pissed all over the football lot. They were proper sporting heroes in the 70s and 80s; and they were plastered most of the time away from the table.

It's funny how the BBC never shows highlights of Higgins any more. Elena and I are snooker fans, and you hardly ever see footage of him. He refused to keep his trap shut and he was a wild-card, but without him snooker wouldn't be what it is today. He broke the door down and the rest just cleaned up after him. It's a disgrace. I like that quote from Jeffrey Bernard about Jimmy White – 'He looks like a man who has seen trouble.' You can't say that about lads nowadays; about Beckham and Lampard. They look like they've just got ready for bed after polishing off their mam's supper on a Sunday night.

Once we'd nailed *Hex* and returned from that tour of Australia and New Zealand we went back to the eighth wonder of the world – Rochdale – to record *Room to Live* (1982).

It's a very underrated album, if you ask me. I think it has one of the best album covers. Good picture of us on the front with a dog. I think that was the same dog that wolfed Karl's passport. Actually, I'm not such a big fan of dogs. I prefer cats.

There's a good mate of mine who drinks around Prestwich. He'll be out every day, unlike me. We used to hang around together in the late 70s/early 80s; getting pissed and stoned and whathavya. He's a lovely bloke. He goes everywhere with his dog. He can only drink in certain pubs, because of his dog. He's a bit of a pub philosopher; the sort who always has a question or an answer for you. He's a good talker, but unlike most pub philosophers he knows what he's going on about. You don't need to look far for your lyrics when you've got characters like that in your local.

People have a funny relationship with their dogs. Blokes in the 80s used to buy them because they were soft cunts and wanted to look hard – you'd see them prancing around with these slavering beasts, these sharks on leads. It seems to be on its way back, all that shit. There's no real need to have something like that around the house, is there? It's a bit disturbing. Cats are much brighter. I used to have quite a few of them around that whole *Room to Live* period.

I was living near Heaton Park. The Pope came to visit the park in 1982; that's where the song 'Papal Visit' on *Room to Live* originated from.

I was in the top flat for a couple of weeks before I moved on. I could see all these Jesuits in the gardens below, rooting through the trees for bombs and things. But the best part was when this Loyalist from Belfast ran at the Pope with this big butcher's knife. All these bishops and cardinals struggled him to the ground. He'd come flying out of The Ostrich pub, just over the road from the park. He was pissed out of his head, draped in a flag – I think he'd just swiped a rugby flag off the wall – Sedgley Park rugby!

It's a big Catholic area, Prestwich. The last thing they wanted to see was this Geoff Capes type with a load of lager in his gut and a kitchen sword in his hand. It was a very sensitive period. What with the Falklands and job shortages . . . I said at the time that people need stimulation more than ever when things are that fucked up. You can't buckle when it gets rocky like that.

But I wasn't in the minority when I stuck up for the army in the Falklands; not in the pubs, anyway. The music industry and the press just saw it as another 'Narky Mark' stance. They had no pride, that was the bottom line. They were only socialists when it suited them. They were like your classic Christian: cunt all week and then a saint on Sunday. I was more of an active socialist than all of them put together. And that goes for the people who I drank with as well.

Weekend socialists, that's what they were. You'd never get them hiring people from outside of London; or if you did it was in a similar vein to that Lenny Bruce joke about the token black man at the party. They didn't have to worry about paying wages to a bunch of lads who hadn't a penny to steal. For all my so-called badness I always make sure the group get their dough.

I can't abide all that forced liberalism. In a strange way they're like fascists: walled off in their own little groups, not listening to people if they're slightly right-wing. How closeted is that?

I hope this book turns out like *Mein Kampf* for the Hollyoaks generation.

I think Kay's part around this period has been overlooked. She was like a financial wizard. Totally on the ball. She wouldn't take any shit. She was up on all the shenanigans.

The whole ethos of the music business is built on outside manipulation. It's borderline criminal. If you don't keep your eye on this, that and the other you find yourself in a terribly murky place. You need people behind you, like a platoon. That's what a lot of people don't understand. That's where a lot of the arguments begin. Too many of them couldn't get their heads around this. We don't operate like most everybody else. I'm not your standard front man. My job's not finished when I walk off the stage, or finish a vocal recording.

Kay was the first one to realize that something was amiss at Kamera; that things weren't tallying up as they should. She had it right as well, as they went bust soon after. I was a bit gutted about that. They had the right idea there.

All this meant that we had to fuck off back to Rough Trade, which I was very unhappy about. It felt like going back to a job that you'd confidently walked out of six months ago, telling everybody about the lucrative future that lay in wait; only to find yourself back there six months later, looking like a prize pillock. Not that I felt like a prize pillock . . . Sometimes you've got to bite the bullet in these situations. It's all experience.

The main beef I had with Rough Trade was that I've never been able to relate to that indie attitude. It's not in my nature to embrace mediocrity, or defeat even – to be content with a *record deal*. There's a lot to be said for one, I'm not knocking that, but if you're good enough you can get a deal anywhere. The point is to take it further, and not solely in a monetary sense.

It's too easy and safe to follow on from where you left off, to listen to the sycophants and the detractors. They're there for a reason. It's the same everywhere. People are beaten down by bogus wisdom every day, bogus notions of management. You only have to look at those two violent Fagins – George Bush and Tony Blair – to see that. This all came about in the mid 90s, when everybody revolted and became their own boss; setting up all these shitty businesses and treating their staff worse than a so-called proper boss.

But I know that only a handful of people can truly tell me something worthwhile, and that'll do me.

I see where they're coming from when they're advising me to go solo or to sit down and just write. Because it's a job in itself keeping your eye on new knives in your back, on vendettas and vampires from the past. It's a carnival of wolves out there. I know the people telling me this are looking out for me. And I do appreciate it – more than they think, probably. But they're missing the point.

In a way, I don't have a choice. I've hung on in there this long, so why fuck off now? That's all part of who The Fall are anyway: the persistent effort that goes into it, the coping, the getting by, and the times when the group's tiptop and you go and have a drink. It's all as one.

Voices 3

All he does is barge in barking orders after he's had a few. He's a total fraud ... He's not a particularly nice man ... We were all fucked up on that tour ... He has a lot of different sides, you see. I'm not with him as another hanger-on. He's helped us out loads of times. He took us on tour when no other fuckers gave a fuck about us ... I can hear them again. Word salads. I'm this, this and this ... The dogs leap with their tongues. And then back down on thin legs ... I come back to a TV unwatched ... They're a grind to be around. But someone must become the bloodhound ... Frontiers. Reparations. Guilt ... Going to the grave with all those unlived lives inside of them ... Asexual desert heads ... Still '80. Still wanting it as it was then. Fixed ... There's only so much you can look at yourself. Before simple insanity ... The retarded consistency of their nagging ... Journalist thief stick. Fat for cash. More dough than his subjects ... It does you good a bit of food; keeps you going. Through the lowlights of the day ... He went for him. Tried to strangle ... First time I met him he walked up to the van and said you're the psychedelic drummer I've been hearing about, then, eh ... And walked back inside. He does a lot more good than people say, though. He knew I was down. He just got on the phone and said I need that kit behind me again. I'll always appreciate that ... The burden of disappearance. Escape in water. Walking sick ... CCTV knows more than most ... This cough seems to be telling me to stop smoking ... Failed to acknowledge the crowd. Angry crowd. Crowd unhappy at being ignored ... I couldn't be arsed hanging around. I thought they were supposed to be on at 10.00. It's not the first time. It's not asking much. All he has to do is lay off the pop for an afternoon. He's fucking it up ... I'm falling asleep in a big car and it's not fucking England ... I'm awake in a big car and it's not fucking England ... Body fogged in cruel uncertainty. In the space of a day suddenly you know nothing ... He was nobody. He was a tumbleweed ... I'm back in the pub. Whistling. He's waiting for me again; dictaphone at the ready. Pedantic fucker ... At least it's flowing better this time. I'll wing him some dust. I'll wing him and watch. I'll sit whiskyed. Make light of his heavy questions ... Perhaps it's me, but I am still drunk. I'm writing this just after the gig. The traffic was really bad. I wish they'd play all the tunes that I like. That beer we had was good, wasn't it, Totale? I've watched them now for nigh on thirty-nine years and never have I encountered such a ... Is it me or is Rob's head the next to roll ... I hope so. There's no place for beards in The ... This is the worst line-up since ... And why has he asked for the forum to be closed down ... What happened to freedom of speech? I can't believe he's asked for the forum to be closed down. Just because he's not that way inclined . . . Bus station café stares. On my wedding day as well . . . The young obese. I'm hearing about you all the time. Hungry kids are new. I never saw them when I was a kid. The young obese. I'm hearing about you all the time . . . Back on the Whyte and Mackay. Only tonight. I'll share it with him. He's not a bad lad . . . There's too many books. I'm now another . . . Lord of the urban jungle . . . I'd rather watch traffic signs than The Fall . . . Surly . . . Curmudgeonly . . . I train-surfed myself once. Heard Knut Hamsun had done likewise. It cleared his cough. Up there on top of the train. The wind. That'll see to your cold. I got up there myself. Felt great. Not like the spare cunt who set on fire . . . Prestwich Clough. Rafters . . . A 70s Manchester. Then 80s. And 90s. And a now that isn't quite so . . . 'Identity cards. But nobody's got a fucking identity. They're all Robbie Williams-ites and Graham Nortons.' '97 humour. Ideas of fun border on retarded . . . And you're on a plane with people you know are out for what they can get . . . But still you pump on. Past the darkling. It's my job to find out what lies at the end of the night . . . More brown bills unpaid . . . Plague-irists . . . Guess-timates . . . I miss my dead mates. I see only trawl ends. And coarse grass . . . Meet you in The Forresters . . . 'If it gets any livelier in here it'll break out into a funeral.' Diamond takes preference over Stella. Rare . . . 'Bird in the Hand'. I don't understand the rules of Killer. Pool-keen blokes making it up. Delaying night and the wife . . . I'm somewhere in England. I've seen a lifetime of pylons. Duped by faulty car clocks. Road maps . . . I'll open a can. Pass them round . . . In chaotic times all clichés are true. And Kung Po King Prawn . . . Nick Cave appeals to surly virgins. Always corduroy . . . Disconnected. All they have in common is food. Talk of last night's food. Bland porn. Black trees. Keep left where possible except when you are overtaking . . . Driving when you are tired greatly increases your accident risk . . . our . . . accident . . . risk . . . Skinny . . . Brittle . . . Rhythms . . . Blackburn night . . . Tomorrow Wigan . . .

11. The Wife

Women are more in tune with rhythms than men. It's very hard being in an all-male group. They don't get anything I say to them. The tunes in my head don't go past three chords. But men can't get it. There's something in their brain that's out of touch with this idea. I always feel alienated from men musically, whereas women can transform my ideas into reality a lot more accurately.

The Slits were great at knocking out stuff like that, until they turned reggae. But with a lot of groups who have female members it's just the 'icing on the cake', so to speak. Eye candy. Get a female bass player – that'd be good! It's amazing how sexist these so-called liberal newspapers are, too – 'So that's why you've got so and so in the band.' No, it's because she can play the fucking flute, you idiot! Or because she can sing better than some daft bastard from Manchester who sounds like a coalminer shouting down a pit. That's why they're in the group.

But it's incorrect to say that Brix smoothed the rough edges off the band. People only said that because of the way she looked.

It wasn't my idea to rope her into the band. I didn't really want my wife in the band. But she came on tour with us and as we needed a guitarist she ended up in the band. There's a lot of shit that needs clearing up about that whole period. For a start, I don't know where the idea originated from that we were rolling in it. We might have had a little more dough than usual, after the relative success – if you can call it that – of 'Victoria' and 'There's a Ghost in My House', but I've never been rolling in it. It's all been distorted. What with that and the idea that

Brix glammed us up – that was actually my idea. It's an old Salford thing – if you're skint, don't let them know you are. That's what that period was about. It wasn't as if we were having monthly number ones, playing Wembley and all that.

I've always tried to dress smart. It's important. There's no need to look like a demick, you don't have to. Primark sells some alright stuff at a fair price. Go and shop there; you don't want to be walking around like an urban scarecrow. Nobody takes a scruff seriously, that's one thing I've learned. It's all fine dressing in this anti-fashion style if you're on the piss in Camden Town, but imagine doing business with a berk dressed like a vagrant . . . It just doesn't work.

I remember my jumper being a big thing all of a sudden. The *NME* ran a story about my Armani jumper, and how Brix had altered the appearance of the once purposefully unimmaculate loudmouth. What a joke! They started losing it then, the *NME*. Started revelling in tittle-tattle. It's come full circle now because they influenced the celebrity mags and now they're aping the celeb mags themselves.

I don't have anything to do with her any more. I hear second-hand that there's an interview with her somewhere and she's always Brix Smith – even though we're no longer married.

What amazes me is what interests the journalists about this. About her boutique or her new line in fashion or whatever it is that month – 'Brix, who used to be married to so-and-so, ex-guitarist of The Fall . . .' What's that got to do with her new range of trilbys? It's a curious world when this sort of thing is read with interest.

I've always believed very strongly in marriage. There's nothing worse than living with a woman if you're not married – from my experience, anyway. Because they're never sure what's going on. I'm conservative with a small 'c' in these matters. For a start, you don't get fucked over as much – you can say, 'That's my wife,' and blokes will leave her alone. And she feels alright too. All the time I've lived with women it's been a case of, 'I'm going to do this . . .' and I'll say, 'Well, I'm going to do that.' And nobody knows where they are. It's alright if you're single and fancy-free and you just have a bird in for a couple of days. I've done all that shit. I just don't think it's fair on the woman.

I don't judge people by their looks. You'd never meet anybody if you did – that's my philosophy. What's the point of only hanging around with people that look like you? Nobody looks like me, anyway. They're all the same actually – all different but the same: hippies and Goths and all the others.

It's intelligence with me. It's not physical. None of that 'opposites attract' shit, either. I think you can waste a lot of time believing tosh like that. I think I'm quite unusual in this respect. It doesn't turn me on at all, that page three sort of shit. Never did as a kid, even. I don't understand it. All that voyeurism is beyond me. It gets to a point where people are sustaining themselves on a shallow diet of cheap pleasures. There's no longevity in it. After a time it dies down, and then they go out looking for the next kick. It's all a bit soulless.

You can't walk down the street without being subjected to some soft-core porn image selling something; or you go to the newsagents and you're bombarded with those awful men's magazines with these shiny women on the cover. Let's be honest here – it's all a bit second-rate. They're not that far removed from those porn mags I used to lift and flog on as a kid; only difference being that those contained some decent articles. Not like the muck that's plastered between the pages of these other things. I know the type of people who work on them. They're a new breed of English frat-boy who gets off on shit updates of *Porky's*; they're like the thick younger brothers of the *Loaded* writers in the 90s, and that's saying something! The only way they can get women is to do a stint on these trashy rags. The worst part is the shit humour they're underpinned with. At least the *Daily Sport* can be quite amusing sometimes. But not the randy college boys; they're the enemies of humour.

Every woman I've been out with has been different. But when we've broken up it's always been for the best. More often than not, they've left me. It's never bothered me, though. Most blokes go suicidal, but not me. Sitting in the pub all day, moping . . . I don't think they should be allowed in pubs – a landlord once said that to me. 'Get these male divorcees out of my pub! They're making everybody miserable.' Sat with one pint all night . . .

'Cheer up, mate.'

'But she's left me.'

'Good, you should be happy.'

It's quite weird, the feedback I get off people in broken relationships or in prison or on their deathbed. They find The Fall's music more stimulating than that usual crap. I find that pretty satisfying. I think it's because it makes them think a bit; it takes their mind off things. A lot of people have said that to me.

I mean, if you're dying and somebody plays you a track by The Police it's not going to stimulate you or console you, is it? One bloke who'd done ten years for manslaughter told me that The Fall had kept him going, kept him together throughout his stay while everybody else would be watching *Top of the Pops*. That was the highlight of the week – all the lifers gathering round to watch *Top of the Pops*. That's punishment in itself. He also told me he'd been wrongly accused as well. Poor chap.

It's been said that I tend to write from an asexual perspective. There's a few love songs in there, but mostly I'd rather leave that to everybody else. It's all been said before. I don't see it as being asexual as such. It's more akin to putting yourself in other people's shoes.

I've got a good talent for that.

I don't want to be like the other lot – Mick Jagger and fucking Rod Stewart. My sex life actually went down when I formed The Fall. It wasn't the reason why I did it, of course. But a lot of people do form groups for money and sex. It's still true today, no matter how avant-garde they claim to be. I was earning more money on the docks, and I had more women. In fact, there have been occasions when I've been getting on with a woman very well and as soon as she found out I was in The Fall she went right off me. I've even tried to cover it up sometimes.

There was this one occasion where I was chatting a girl up in a pub near me and doing really well. But she kept saying, 'I know you from somewhere.' I thought she might have seen me on telly or something. But I didn't want to mention The Fall. I'm asking her if she wants to come back to my place or should we go back to hers, and then she started talking about one of my sisters, saying she used to knock about with her. It turns out I'm related to her. I should have realized. She had the same nose as me; the Smith nose.

Elena's the best thing to have happened to me in some time.

I met her in the Volks Bar in Berlin; this old circular bar. It's a great place. She was promoting one of our shows. She used to put on a lot of hip-hop stuff too. Her musical tastes are a lot different from mine – Cool Keith and the real hip-hop before it went stupid, when it was much more adventurous, and less mainstream, like The Sugarhill Gang.

I think she was a fan of The Fall as well, though.

This would have been in 1996 – which was quite a rocky time for me – because I knew her for about three or four years before we'd started going out.

We hit it off from the start, but she was in Berlin and all that. I saw her again three or four years later. She used to ring me up occasionally. Then one day I just got on a plane to Berlin and thought, she's the one for me, and proposed to her in 2000. She just looked at me – who's this weird guy? What are you doing here?

There came a point when I had to work out what I was doing – not that I had a load of choices. It was instinctive. I was on my own and didn't have a lot of dough; scrimping to pay the band and bills. And when it came down to it, I knew she was the best for me.

She's got a good sense of humour, that's very important. And she shares my love of literature. I think she's very underrated as a musician. She's not over-educated on the keyboards. She knows the basics. Coming from a dance and hip-hop background helps a lot – there's a real drive to those incessant rhythms. Ask a fellow to play a bass riff over and over again, they get bored and start embellishing it because they think it should have another twelve notes in it. Women can do it and make it exciting.

She deals with things well. I've had other women in the group and they've been completely doolally. After a couple of gigs they're on the verge of an emotional collapse.

She has a good eye for things, too – the outsider's viewpoint. It's very handy. They see things as a whole and not in pieces, like those who have lived here all their life. Germany has probably the greatest educational system I've ever come across. I was never one for school, but the methods they use seem extremely effective. A bit like Scottish people – they've been taught properly. They can be objective and they can comment on things constructively. It might have something to do with the war; whereas with the British some of them still have this in-built imperialistic viewpoint that they know everything – Tony Blair, for instance. They'd rather interfere with somebody else's life instead of addressing what's on their own doorstep. Even the daftest Germans read books all day. They've read everything. Even the roadies. Not like the Brits at the Reading Festival, where *Mojo* is the tome of choice. The barman might be a big fucking Bavarian but when he's not serving he'll read a book. It's important. If people read more, they'd come to a better understanding of other people and there'd be less people trudging off to shrinks.

I remember going to a further education college for six weeks to do A-level English, two years after I left school. This English teacher I had was supposed to be one of the best in Manchester. Not a fuddy-duddy: a young girl. It was all mixed ages in this class, and she's asking me what I've read, and I'm going – Norman Mailer, Nietzsche, Raymond Chandler. She hadn't heard of any of them. Norman Mailer! She hadn't heard of him because he's American; and she's supposed to be one of the best English teachers in Manchester. Never heard of William Burroughs. It's all Jane Austen and Dickens, Shakespeare and Thomas Hardy – which is all good. But it's a poor show when a so-called English expert hasn't any knowledge of Norman Mailer. Even a German dog would know who he is.

It seems like you have to be of a certain type to get on nowadays. There's no savvy in-between – in the media and in education, anyway. In one corner you've got those brainless magazine jockeys; and then there's the embittered cynic in his mid thirties who's been stripped of all passion and sees through everything, even himself – they like them on the *Guardian*. And then again there's the festival type who floats around looking pretty and not offending until she's worth a mint for no other reason than being pretty and inoffensive – Jo Whiley gave birth to these pointless butterflies. These are the reasons for articles about Brix's new carpet. It's disappointing when programmes about moving cushions and painting kitchens are watched by more than nine people. I think they should have a yearly clear out of staff. Keep it fresh, like The Fall.

I have a clear out literally every year. I hire a big, yellow skip that sits proudly outside next to the cars, and in it I throw everything that's surplus. This can be all sorts – clothes, records, books. I don't like clutter. I can't work amid clutter. I crave space. Whenever I'm coming to the end of an album I'll spread out all the lyric sheets on the floor in an empty room and stand over them, all the time working out the correct order of play – a bit like a director when they're looking at the storyboard of the film. I don't know how people can work in confined spaces.

It's no wonder so many mistakes are made in the modern office. They're filled with too many bodies. How can you concentrate fully and correctly when you're sat in the middle of thirty voices and bodies all vying for attention? It's the modern incarnation of the industrial workhouse. It's frightening, like Pink Floyd's worst middle-class nightmares writ large. We're all part of a machine. I never knew this. Now I feel enlightened!

There's a lot to be said for de-cluttering one's life.

A funny thing happened to me a couple of years ago when I was cleaning out. A mate of mine had sent me all these old newspapers from World War Two. I'm filtering through them, reading the odd line here and there about the Blitz and what-havya; and then all of a sudden I felt tired and went to bed. As I'm getting in bed I heard this crashing sound; part of the doorway had caved in. I was literally minutes away from being under a load of bricks. Imagine if they'd found me beneath all this rubble among a load of newspaper clippings dating back to the Blitz; they'd have probably thought I'd been there since the 40s.

But if you want to get your work done, if you want to be an artist, it's a good first step to avoid clutter. I only have three chairs in the house, for instance; one for the wife, one for me, and one for a guest. No more. One guest at a time – that's my philosophy. You don't want your house turning into a hippy commune. You'll never get anything done if that's the case. It's vital that you lay down rules like that when you're working from home; because it can get quite difficult otherwise.

I've always needed space to write, even as a kid. I couldn't sit downstairs with the rest of my family. I'd have to be alone in my room.

It's like when I wrote that short story for *City Life* magazine. They put me in a writer's office in the *Manchester Evening News*. It was fucking great: big typewriter, lock on the door. I whacked out a four-page short story in two hours. No distractions, just a cup of tea now and again. It was amazing. No telly. No phones. No books – very 60s-like. There was nothing to go out of the door for – all that lay outside the door was a mile of typists. I like to get in a flow with things. I can do it with songs. But there's always something, like some wanker will ring up. It can send you nuts. Then you return to it and you've had it; you end up with a mediocre version.

So you have to try and box yourself off.

I do this on stage, too. I like to create space. That's what a lot of those hand movements are for. It's a performance, after all. And I'm at my best when I'm in control of my immediate surroundings. It was the same when I used to talk in between songs, tell funny stories. I suppose I was a bit influenced by Lenny Bruce, but it was also because other bands were really po-faced and earnest. There was no performance there. I couldn't see the point of it. I'm not talking about end-of-the-pier shit – just a few anecdotes here and there; a bit Lenny Bruce, a bit Bernard Manning.

That's what I liked about early Iggy Pop. His performances were very much part of the whole thing. You could take the music out of it – not that you'd want to do that – and it'd still work in a weird way.

The problem I had was that the group started playing louder than me, drowning me out. When people are starved of attention, or they think they're playing second-fiddle, they'll revolt in some way or another after a bit. I've had that a lot. You're dealing with kids when that sort of thing occurs. They can't see that it's a whole; can't see their own contribution; don't understand that they're not me, and I'm not them. I don't whinge about not playing the guitar or the drums. When I fiddle around with their amps, it's because it needs to be done. I must be hearing it different to them. But you'd be surprised by how many people tell me that it works. Not that I need telling. I know it works. They don't realize that I'm hearing it as a whole because I've not got my head stuck in an instrument.

I keep going on about it, but musicians are a unique sort. The stage is everything to them – there's nothing outside of it. It's as if they're still performing in a school play and their mam's out in the audience and they're busting a gut to upstage every other fucker around them. I've got to keep an eye on this all the time.

I've heard people say that I've got too close to some of the lads I've had in my group, that they start relying on me like a second dad. They said that about Ben, for instance. But I don't think I did. I was just being me. The problems start when *they* start buying into all that shit and then I have a go at them because they've played like a toddler on vodka. And their heads drop and the annoyance grows into full-time hatred.

It's no wonder that I've never had kids myself. There's still time. But I don't think you should bring a kid into the world if you can't feed it. I've always thought that. People look at you like you're mad. I couldn't have had a kid when I was twenty-one. I didn't know whether I was going to do another LP, for one thing. The rest of the group were different, even though they were younger than me: '*Grotesque* is number 1 in the indie charts and oh, by the way, I'm a daddy.'

And I'm thinking, 'You're only nineteen, man, you don't think *Grotesque* is going to finance you for the next twenty-five years, do you, because it's not?' But you don't say that.

It's what you get from coming off a big family – I've seen it all. There's nothing that shocks me. I resent people thinking that I'm too frightened or impotent to have kids.

A lot of people say I'd be a really good dad. But I'm the sort who'd forget about the child. I'd be at the pub engrossed in a conversation when I should be at home because the baby's in front of the fire getting slowly roasted. I'm that type of fellow.

12. The Devil's Compass

It was a typical Brix evening. We were in Los Angeles among writers who were all chewing cheeks on chokey and talking themselves up. It was some house party or other. Tight-fisted bastards hadn't bought enough booze in. The so-called hell-raisers were sipping champagne. I've seen more hellraising on a Sunday in Prestwich. They couldn't drink. They were still acting seventeen, feigning drunkenness.

Most of them had been at some arts college in Vermont, and they seemed like charlatans to me. Read any of their books and it's as if they've photocopied the first two pages 230 times, done a line and bunged it to the publishers. And the publishers are so happy that they've got one of the so-called Brat Pack in their ranks, they've gone and said, 'Awesome!' This is how careers are built.

It's all padding around one or two semi-good ideas.

But because they're there in their full glory, you're supposed to tell him how much you like his book and tell her what a good ending her book has, and so on. And because I'm not half as belligerent as I'm made out to be, I just kept my trap shut and waited for it all to finish. But I remember thinking, what a cotton-wool world they live in. They were all variations on the same theme: totally unable to move on from flimsy stories about cocaine and other stuff. Even at the time I remember thinking that they'll never find a different perspective. You read their stuff now, and it's nothing more than another 1980s counselling session on the page. Who wants to read that? We're talking about the elite here. The opportunities at their disposal were ridiculous. And most just spurned them and chose to shoot junk instead. Daft bastards. That's the background that she comes from.

I've had it with all the talk about the so-called classic era of The Fall; the Brix era, etc. I'm not rankled by it. I just think it's been documented so much there's no point reclaiming it for the purpose of this book. It was over twenty years ago, remember – let's not unearth more dull memories.

People have got a serious problem if they're interested in wading through it again. I don't think it's the best era. I don't even like the word 'era' – it's very *Mojo* terminology; as if I've come to an end.

I'm always dissatisfied with the way things pan out. That's what keeps me going. It's like that film *Last Days*, based on Kurt Cobain, which reminds me of the Sartre quote, 'Hell is other people.' It's true. It's a good film. You can see how he was driven crackers by his mad wife and his flimsy mates. They're all living in this mansion, and he's hiding away in one of the ten bedrooms, holding his shotgun, or he's traipsing around the gardens mumbling. I don't think it had anything to do with his heroin habit. Everything had caved in on him and he had bad taste in mates. I don't think he'd ever been in the company of good people.

You see his lickspittle mates arrive in this isolated group, fried out of their minds. But when he's fucked up, they all piss off in a car. And then they come back a few days later and they keep doing that until he's blown his brains out. He can't stand it. He's trying to play his guitar and write his lyrics and they're all whispering among themselves, right in front of him. And I've seen that with the groups that I've had. I just kick them in the arse, but him being him he's too shy to say anything about it. And he's got to deal with the rent collectors and some fundamentalist mitherer.

Meanwhile, one of these fellows, one of his so-called mates, is singing along to 'Venus in Furs' all the time. And he can't handle it; all of it's making him worse. And the minute they see the police come to check everything out they get in a car and leave him to rot. They don't give a shit about him, it's obvious.

Another thing I'm reminded of is the film of *Rising Damp*. I'm a big fan of Leonard Rossiter and Rigsby, and the series itself had a lot more depth to it than people think. Pale-minded liberals have moaned the subtleties out of it, as is their wont. Rigsby wasn't all that bad. He's not the bigoted tyke he's been made out to be. He's just a bloke from another generation – a lost sort, looking for company.

It's interesting, because at the end of the film circumstances force the other characters into revealing themselves. They've all been acting behind his back, playing out these powerful visions of themselves with Rigsby as their focus of derision; but in truth he's at the centre of a sly sham. In the end they stand revealed as bullshitters and con men. In comparison he's nowhere near as calculating and untrustworthy.

I can relate to things like that.

In any walk of life it's hard to filter out the charlatans from the good sort. It's a curse. The amount of vultures who have dealt dishonestly behind my back doesn't bear thinking about. When The Fall are at their best, we're like a platoon.

The longer I've been around, the more I've just learned to take my time about things. In the beginning I was quite sensitive. I didn't have the right head on to deal with the cretins and cockroaches. I was too busy perfecting the moody writer thing. That can be a real problem. As soon as I started to fill in tax forms and sort paperwork out, as soon as I didn't have five days to be artfully glum and existential, all that changed. But at the start I couldn't get to grips with the rock world, with the whole rigmarole and the leeches at the centre of it. When you're caught up in something that has no grace, it makes sense to take verbal revenge.

It does get you down sometimes, but there's no point wallowing in it. A lot of stuff on *Perverted by Language* (1983) came out of one of those low periods that I tend to have. Kay had left and the band had changed again. That's not to say I wasn't excited by it.

It's a suburban album. You just have to look at some of the titles – 'Neighbourhood of Infinity', 'Garden'. But it's not The Jam or anything. They were more BBC2, with a couple of 'angry' lyrics thrown in.

The difference with me is that I always find the present more real than any other period from my life. I know this isn't the case with a lot of other writers, who spend more time regressing than tackling the here and now. I prefer to look at LPs more as contemporary chronicles.

Walking the same places, skint, you see a lot of hidden sores when you're having an off day. Your eyes have changed and the simple actions of other persons take on a significance that may or may not be truly there. These are extreme moments.

That's the feeling behind the album.

Scratch the surface of English suburbia and you'll see a bored bloke looking back at you asking what you're up to. We're not talking David Lynch here, it's not as lurid as that. But that makes it all the more interesting. Like, why is that person peering out of his window so early in the morning anyway?

It seemed to me that people started spending an unusual amount of hours meddling with their lawns and privets. Rinsing the paving and touching up the paintwork on their window frames. I'd be walking around wondering how I could finance everything and there'd be a fellow in an ill-fitting pair of slacks adding dabs of white paint to the white paint that was already there. Killing time. Or I'd be sat in the pub and grown men would suddenly start talking loudly about their plans for an extension or how the new curtains are looking.

But instead of getting it down in a straight-up way, I threw in a Lindsay Anderson feel to it all. I'm a big fan of his stuff. The best thing he did, *Britannia Hospital*, gets overlooked in favour of *If . . .*, but it's great. There's a load of shit going on in the hospital with the managers and doctors; all totally inept and scatty. Really, the film's just a barbed pop at the government and the times. On one side of the wall you had the garden lot, and they were okay, and then you had families who'd been shunted into these tower blocks like a rat experiment. Thatcher got blamed for it, but in truth it was the socialists who built them. Mike Leigh nailed it in *Meantime*: lads at loose ends and lifts not working, the neighbours barking through the non-walls. It was a nightmare – a daymare. I had girlfriends who lived in these places and you'd sit down and look around and they're all the same – wallpaper, carpet, even the smell. Prison-life. They had their own awful presence. I feel sorry for anybody who's had to endure anything like that. It was a terrible time.

Other bands were resorting to love songs, as is always the case in uncertain times: sugared denial. But I'm incapable of putting a new spin on the love idea. I don't know what else could be written about the subject. Maybe if you wrote it from the perspective of one musician I know of. I hear that he'd been having a written correspondence with Rose West a few years ago and she wanted to take it a bit further. I should float that idea around.

Something more accurate than fiction – that's what I was trying to get at with *Perverted by Language*. I think you can only get at reality like that in a jarred and abstract way. It sounds ridiculous but I find it has more reality to it than something polished and linear.

It's not a very well-liked LP. People find it claustrophobic. But it's not always about making music in the traditional sense of the word. Sometimes it's right to try to create a new, imaginary world. There's some great noises on that record, and I think it works a bit like a short-story book.

It's better than Echo and the Bunnymen and all the rest of

the gonks around at that time. Indulging in depression, like it's a lifestyle choice . . . I hated that. I've always wanted The Fall to be the group that represents people who are sick of being dicked around; those that have a bit of fight in them.

The cover's the best thing for most people. It's a bit like that Hogarth engraving *Gin Lane*. It's important you get it right with covers, that they reflect what's contained within. I've never really had a problem. *The Light User Syndrome* and the American version of *Reformation* are the only two I can think of that I reckon should have been done again. I look fucking terrible on *Light User* – I wasn't eating my greens, and my mouth was wearing whisky perfume. *Reformation* was the work of Bob Gruen. He took that famous picture of Lennon with his arms crossed wearing that New York City T-shirt. He's done everybody. Sadly, they're all dead or nearly dead. I'm walking around his studio in New York and his walls are caked in coffin dwellers. In my opinion, he's still living off all his old pictures. I mean they're good pictures and everything, but his eye has obviously had its day. The cover looks like a poxy school picture, or a prison Polaroid taken for the family back at home by the screws who have loosened up a bit after a couple of Christmas cans. I don't know what they were thinking when they packed us off to his studio. They should have just stuck our heads on that painting called *The Hustler* – the one with the cats and dogs smoking and drinking and playing pool. That would have made more sense.

It's a pain in the arse getting covers sorted out nowadays. In the past I'd just hand them the artwork and say, 'Use that!' and they'd go off and knock it out in a day or two. All they've got to do is follow instructions. But it's not as easy as it sounds. There'll be three girls who have worked on it for four weeks or so. It's like with 'Reformation!', the single off the album: they must have sent me about twenty-five shots of how it might turn out.

'Here's the cover for your perusal, Mr Smith.'

Not even different covers – just little changes here and there, different lettering. It reminded me of a Dulux colour co-ordinator – 'You can have the fireplace like this and you can have your walls like this and this shade complements your shed perfectly.'

Instead of sending me three or four vastly different ideas, they send me twenty-five of the same . . . You're looking at it wondering, what's the difference? When I used to do the covers I'd just take a photo and get them to blow it up 12 × 12. All they've got to do is follow the instruction that I've written out for them, but they're incapable. For some odd reason *they* think *they* know best. It'd be a different matter if the boss imposed some ideas on them; but because it's Mad Mark they flip out. And the results are wop. In their eyes they're breaking new ground with twenty-five identical images. You don't want to have a go at them too much. But it needs saying . . .

Simple fact is, there's a great divide between a graphic designer and an artist. Graphic designers only know how to use a computer – they're the visual equivalent of an audio typist. They bounce out of college with very boring ideas. I'd rather do it myself than hand it over to one of them. They're too in control of what they're doing, they have to be – it's a fucking computer after all. That's why it doesn't flow as it should.

I've noticed that a lot of new covers are poor imitations of the stuff that Peter Saville did in the 80s. All very minimal and cool. It was good when he did it, but not so good when it's Ben or Luke with his new computer and he's trying to pass it off as his own. There's nothing wrong with being influenced by somebody, that's all part of the process. I'm not that naive. But there comes a time when your own ideas have to take precedence.

The other thing is: kids getting music off computers. They're missing out there. It's all too immediate and empty. For one, it's not tangible. This sounds a bit romantic, but you're losing out with that shit. That's why artwork's not seen as it used to be. It's just one more throwaway component. I've got a feeling it'll come back, though; same with vinyl. I still think in terms of vinyl – sides one and two. It's funny, because there'll be somebody on the other end of the phone saying, 'Side one and two? But we're talking about a CD.' And I'll be ranting away, totally oblivious, saying, 'I want side one like this and side two like that – now sort it out!'

It helps to be in the know . . .

A lot of European painters listen to The Fall when they're working: both bad and good. It appeals to them a lot. It's interesting to me, because I'm not really an art person: I know what I like, etc.

They always seem to feel it a lot more – painters and sculptors. They always say: 'Don't understand you, don't know what you're going on about. I live on an island.' But they get the colours from it and the feeling.

One painter I do like is this lad from Coventry, George Shaw. He does all these landscapes that look just like photographs – Labour Clubs and parks and rows of houses. They're beautifully executed, really evocative. Some of them remind me of the scenery near where I live, places like Heaton Park.

I stuck some of his work in *Reformation*. They're quite intense. He's an old-school craftsman. You can tell he knows what he's doing and why he's doing it. I like paintings that have the feeling of a story, that appear immediate and easy to understand but gradually reveal more telling details.

I get a lot of artists wanting to design our covers. Most of them shit. But there's a few I don't mind. Michael Pollard, who designed *This Nation's Saving Grace*, he was a good bloke. It's a fantastic cover. It's got a good feel to it. Sometimes, things just fall into your lap, like with *Reformation*: it was left up to me to sort the cover out, and I had a few images in my mind, but one day I stumbled across this mosaic that a bloke called Mark Kennedy had done for me as a present, and it punched me in the face as the right image to go with. It has a unique religious feel to it. Quite fitting: we're a faith unto ourselves.

Mark's a mate of mine from Manchester. I've known him a few years. He does the live backdrops as well. He gets commissions from the likes of Noel Gallagher and Beckham's auntie or whatever for his mosaics. But as with a lot of artists he sells them way too cheap. As if these people are skint. They're funny like that, artists. They've got fuck-all business acumen. He'll be telling me about how he's just sold one of his mosaics to Posh for seven quid or something. I'll be saying to him, 'Mark, you shouldn't do that.' But he never listens. What he does is very good. I just think it deserves more money. Most of them don't understand that money is at the centre of it all; more so than in the music world. If you're not flogging your work you're not eating. At least with an album you can flog it and just about live if it doesn't sell. That's the good thing about Damien Hirst; he understood this from the off. He didn't turn his back on it or shy away from it. And now he's worth a mint. That's because the art world didn't know how to cope with his brashness. It's the only way to go about it if you ask me.

After *Perverted* and after Brix joined the group I thought we needed to steer it in another direction. It all got a bit monotonous – maybe that's why it's not as well received as some of the others. There's a difference between plain monotony and creating a syndrome by hitting the same note again and again; when that happens it's great. But plain monotony can get fucking tedious. There's no inflection there. I noticed it with some of Craig's playing. That's why I decided to pop it up a little and alter the rhythms.

I'd be thinking about that sort of thing while sorting through a mound of tax bills. It all got a bit much. That's what you get for not compromising. It's a real test to retain your hunger when you're in deep with all that shit. It's in your head all the time. At the start it's your problem; but then of course it becomes the group's problem. And you try and placate them while getting them to keep their heads together and work on the new LP. It's not easy. I'm surprised we even finished *The Wonderful and Frightening World of The Fall* (1984).

I moved back to where I was brought up around then, as well. I got rid of the vipers, the hangers-on, the piss-and-vinegar lot.

It's a good area. I still live there. Strong Jewish/Irish community. You can't act like a twat. It's got great scenery as well. Bargain Booze is a particular favourite shop of mine. You can get some good offers there.

It's funny when journalists talk about me as a backwoods sort. What they don't realize is that you can't afford to be unenlightened where I come from. I'd like to see how the Notting Hill community would cope if they placed a bunch of immigrants on their doorstep. I happen to think the working class have integrated very well over the years – a hell of a lot more than they're credited for.

I think it relates to the unashamed way I voted Tory back then. That wasn't the done thing. They couldn't understand it. To them, if you're from a working-class background then you have no right doing things like that. It's not about choice with them. They believe you should all think the same, because they do – on the surface, anyway. Inside, they can't abide the proles; they hate to see them get on and it's worse still if they infiltrate their cosy clan.

They couldn't understand that the left and right were never a threat anyway; that the worst thing is a sanitized society ruled by the middle class.

The working class and the real upper class have a lot in

common. They know where they're from, they like a drink, have a sense of humour. It's the middle you need to look out for.

Any left-wing ideas I had had vanished around this point. My ego can deal with the criticism. Ego's all part of the game. If I didn't think like that I would have been eaten up by self-doubt back when the Morleys and Burchills were venting their spleen. The hypocritical part of it is that those fuckers played on their ego just as much as I did. What drove all of those late-70s journalists was the fact they weren't in a band. Looking back, they may have been able to write better sentences than they can today, but the way they hung around the likes of Iggy Pop and Lou Reed and so-and-so was sickening. One year they're shot to hell with some degenerate rock group, talking about nihilism, getting down with the true heart of punk self-destruction; then they're writing about the scourge of Thatcher and the death of communities. It's funny how so many of them have moved to Brighton now. All led by the devil's compass. Cosying up to Fatboy Slim and Chris Eubank over a Sunday roast. It's worse than London. They've created their own modern cultural prison. Burchill and Paul McCartney are the screws!

It started about ten years ago, and now it's a real middle-class retreat. Shit pubs. Shit atmosphere. They think that if they go there they'll all live in harmony away from the moths. It's such a Victorian idea. You can't hide like that. It's the *Guardian*'s version of *The Prisoner*. They're so middle class they put pebbles on the beach so they don't get any sand between their toes. No wonder nothing comes out of it. It's not a patch on Blackpool. That's the real seaside town.

It's the second Iron Circle, after London; you can't come in unless you're making over £40,000 a year and you're a media puppet.

Blackpool, on the other hand, that's a great place to spend a holiday. There's no cultural elitism there, thank fuck. They've got some smashing chip shops as well. It gets a lot of stick for some odd reason. I think it's because it knows what it is — it's not striving to ape elsewhere. I like places that know themselves. Not like Brighton . . . I'd rather have Riley back in the band than live there.

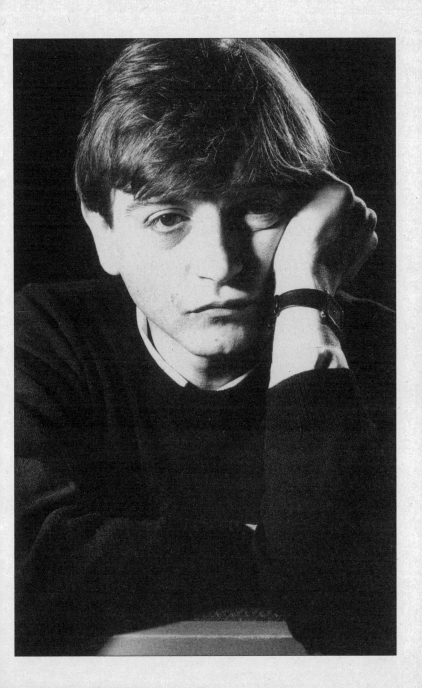

I can't believe it's happening. Two months spent dwelling on my indigestion, and then this, this violent rigmarole. The things you do when skint. 'Youth-Eraser M25'. I'm one of ten now; but there'll be more . . .

13. Death of the Landlords

I was clearing out the other day and I came across a review of *Frenz Experiment*, saying how this could have been great, how it could have been like T-Rex's *Electric Warrior*. I never attempted to make an album like T-Rex. I don't see the point in anybody trying to make an album like T-Rex, although people do. I don't mind it when journalists make fair comparisons, when they've done their homework. But comparing *Frenz* to *Electric Warrior* is plain daft.

Journalists completely lost it around this time, in the mid to late 80s, and have yet to recover. I think it had something to do with the success of *Smash Hits* and *The Face*. Both of them were shit. In one corner you had empty vessels asking you worthless questions about your favourite colour, and then in the other you had these hip bands grassing on their drug dealers in order to get a matchbox-size picture in *The Face*. Suddenly, journalism's all about tat and pictures. Aside from a couple of okay writers, that's all *The Face* was – cool photography. They'd never have us in there, because I once wore a tatty jumper.

Smash Hits did give us one of my favourite reviews, though. I mustn't have a go at them too much.

Singles reviewed by Samantha Fox, 1986
The Fall: Living Too Late (Beggars Banquet)

I didn't like this at all – it's really crappy . . . he sounds like he's been having yodelling lessons. It seems to be the fashion at the moment to like The Smiths and these sorts of groups, and to me the lyrics are really depressing. I heard one the other day while I was in Kensington Market trying on some jeans and it gave me a headache. The Smiths, it was. Singing 'Oh my God, I can't get a job, what am I going to do?' As for this song, I listened to the first half and I had to turn it off. My mother was in the other room and she shouted, 'Nah, I don't like that one – get it off!'

That's as good as it got inside *Smash Hits*: page 3 birds airing their views. I think it's great actually – better than being harangued by Tony Parsons and Julie Burchill.

I've always looked at interviews as being an important part of the game. I very rarely read other groups' interviews but when I do they usually come across tame and irrelevant. The group used to moan about me hogging the limelight in the late 70s/early 80s, but as soon as they were given the opportunity to spew forth they loused it up and ended up sounding like they'd never seen a book or a newspaper in their lives. Hacks and hackettes love all that. They love not being challenged. But with me it's different – totally opposite.

Most journalists believe everything they read. It sounds clichéd but it's the truth. They've got bollocks for brains, and they're lazy. They can't be bothered to verify what's in front of their eyes. They're so distanced from the subjects they're writing about they have to turn to the internet.

And then you turn up for the interview and it's as if you should feel privileged that some Luke or Alex chap is asking you a list of third-rate questions that some other journalist asked you two years ago from the same magazine. It's not always the fault of the person asking the questions; most of the time they're just youngish blokes who can't handle their drink. I blame it on the editors and their passion for revisiting old ground. You only have to look at the people they have on the covers – it's a six-month cycle of accepted icons, like The Beatles and The

Sex Pistols, Neil Young and Pink Floyd. It never changes. I think it's because they're as docile as the audience they're writing for – Tony Blair's flunkies; ageing hippies who smoked too much pot in the 70s; office men with roadie hairstyles who play along to Pink Floyd on their guitars after work. I shouldn't laugh . . . the editors are only looking out for these guys. They have to be reminded why they liked these bands in the first place.

And what's the point of those little interviews I do with them? They're on the phone for about an hour and a half. Then they print a few paragraphs and a picture of me laughing. It's a joke.

It was the same with *Hey Luciani*. They didn't bother to listen to what I was saying and my reasons for writing it. It sailed so far over their heads I might as well have been writing hate mail to their wives.

'But I thought he wrote lyrics. What's he doing writing a play?'

It's astonishing that half of them could even cross the road to actually see it . . .

I wrote it in a blaze. It began as a song for the *Bend Sinister* album and then turned into a play when I went on to write the bulk of it while on tour in America. I'd get back from playing and just get on with it.

It's good to work like that sometimes – to live in two separate worlds. Parts of it were based on David Yallop's book *In God's Name*, about these mysteries surrounding the death of Pope John Paul I, Albino Luciani, in 1978. He'd only been in power for thirty-three days and then he died from a 'heart attack'. But Yallop suggests that there was more to it, because he aimed to eradicate all the corruption at the heart of the Vatican. It wasn't all that earth-shattering to hear something like that, not for me anyway. It's hardly shocking news that the Vatican isn't a beacon of honesty. The really interesting thing about the book is the supporting characters and their ability to deny their involvement.

But, as with most ideas, the more I worked on it the less it had to do with all that shit – the pope, the Vatican, etc. In the end I seem to remember describing it as a cross between *The Prisoner* and Shakespeare. That's how I thought of it at the time anyway. I guess it's better to read it than it is to watch, though – that's what I like about Shakespeare.

It was one of the first instances of the broadsheets covering something that wasn't standard 'Art'. You get it all the time nowadays – pop stars getting reviews in broadsheets. But it was different then. Sure enough, they didn't think much of it, but you're always going to get somebody wanting to do a number on you when you try something completely different. Most of them just thought I was winging it. That's inevitable, especially in the theatre world, which is a Vatican in itself.

But through doing that I met Leigh Bowery. I think he was still doing his thing in Leicester Square in the Taboo nightclub; wearing those outlandish outfits, dancing and singing. I'd already met Michael Clark before *Hey Luciani* when he used some of our stuff for one of his ballets.

I admire the discipline of ballet. You've got to work at it. It's a hard business, both physically and mentally. And Clark was seen as a bit of a maverick. He liked his nights out and whathavya and he was open about it, but he was still very professional. It's similar to the European painters: he felt it more than understood it.

We worked on *I Am Kurious, Oranj*. We adapted the title from a Swedish porno film – *I Am Curious, Yellow*. I was trying to make the point that we all share some kind of common knowledge that's within ourselves; that comes out in all sorts of things. Some people call it a gene pool. It's as if you already know subconsciously about historical incidents. You don't have to have been taught it. It's in-built. At the time I wanted to put this across, basically as a loose explanation of what was happening in Belfast: it's in the head and bones and there's nothing you can do about it.

I was on a roll at that time. I'm rarely short of ideas, and I'm not into preserving them too much, either. If it's in your head and you've got the right people around you, then there's no better time to tell that story. You can't be afraid of reactions when it's like that. I think too many writers hold too much back for another time and then lose the initial spark.

The idea was that Clark would do the ballet side to it and we'd come on and play every now and again. The band was very tight at the time and I reckon we could have played anywhere and delivered.

We took it to the Edinburgh Festival and it was a real punch in the face for the *artistes* and critics. The confidence behind the production threw people; there were no half-measures. It was all very bright and brash, and those that got it really got it. You see it a lot more now in films and on TV, historical fiction depicted in a brazen way. It was never intended to be high art or low art. I don't know what those terms mean, to be honest. It was fuck-all like anything else. That's good enough in itself, if you ask me. I've certainly never seen anything before or since quite like it. I'm not saying it was perfect or brilliant, but I know for a fact that those who did hook into it experienced something special.

Me and Leigh Bowery would slope off for a pint between rehearsals. He was a good fellow like that; none of the other performers came. Just me and Leigh still wearing his makeup and the underclothes to his Heinz baked beans costume. He would stand at the bar in this hilarious get-up ordering two pints and two whiskys, with all these hard-nut Scots staring at him. He didn't give a fuck. He'd just nod to them and sit down.

It was a terrible shame that he died. He was very bright. Never had any money but that never deterred him: a proper artist. It's a real test of somebody's mettle when it's like that. The good ones ride it and come out the other side, not neces- sarily wadded but better at their game. There were a lot of people around that whole Taboo scene who basically cashed in on his big personality, who appropriated a poorer version of him. It always happens with the real originals: the plagiarists are never far behind, waiting to rake it in.

I remember another great character – Fred. He was the land- lord at The Woodthorpe in Prestwich. A funny bastard.

I spent a lot of afternoons talking to Fred. He was great. He'd boot you out if you didn't drink quickly enough. He'd tell you to drink up and get another or leave – a proper landlord.

'Look at him over there,' he'd say, pointing at an old man with an untouched half. 'All afternoon he's been there. He's no good to me. Not like you, Mark.'

We had a band meeting there once, with Ben, Steve and Spencer, and he refused to serve Spencer.

'I don't serve ex-cons.'

Fucking hilarious. All because of Spence's cue-ball bald head. That's the way he was, the last of the good landlords.

He left a few years ago. He got out before the pub got refurbished and became just another concentration camp with taps. It's an important building, over a century old. Joseph Holt, the famous Manchester brewer, used to live there. They wanted to turn it into a nightclub at one stage, but it's written some- where that they can't fiddle around with it too much. It's not what it used to be, though.

I'd sit there watching all the workers rolling in, resenting my presence because I didn't live like them. It's funny how you can be so quickly disliked for ruling your own time. I'm not saying I'm better in any way. I just find it strange that it's such a big deal.

Record companies are the same: they don't like you doing your own thing. When I started up Cog Sinister there was an audible groan of disappointment among them. That might sound strange now, after all the shenanigans I've had with record companies over the years, but it doesn't matter who you are: if you can nail an album a year some fucker will want to sign you. So they weren't best pleased when I started up on my own.

After *Bend Sinister, The Frenz Experiment* and *I am Kurious, Oranj* it dawned on me that the time had come for me to do it myself, to move on. It was all about control again. Maybe the reason why *Seminal Live* (1987) wasn't such a great album is that I had my mind on other things. But that's not to say I deliberately released something that was wilfully shoddy. I've never purposefully knocked out a shit album.

Still, it wasn't a particularly cosy time. Brix and I had pretty much had it with each other, and I wasn't overly enamoured with the Beggars way of doing things. I wanted full control. At the time I thought *Palace of Swords* was a good way of letting people get hold of old Fall stuff. Having ripped up contracts in the past, I was still able to release some of our old recordings which weren't readily available then. All those years of beans and skrimping for cigs were a blessing in disguise in a roundabout way.

Looking back, it's evident now that it was another one of those 'clear out and clear off' periods. Time to grow new bones etc.

Cog Sinister was the first step.

The phrase 'pre-cog' comes from having the ability to see into the future – pre-cognition. I've always felt this. Countless times I've written something or said something and it's manifested itself in reality. I'm not talking standard coincidence. It's more than that, something slightly more sinister – hence the name of the label. I guess you could relate it back to the tarot.

I had an office on Princess Street in Manchester. The idea was I'd go there and write while working on the label side of things. But we're talking Manchester here. As soon as anybody starts anything up in Manchester you've got bodies at your door. I'd go to the offices in the day and John the Postman would be manning the place for me and it'd be rammed with people. It was like a Marx Brothers sketch. You'd have Inspiral Carpets over there and a Shaun Ryder-ite in the other corner. I didn't write a word. I'd just do a swift about turn and fuck off back to the pub, the one place I was supposed to be getting away from.

They weren't on the make as such. They were just looking for a break. You've got to remember that Manchester was little more than a wasteland in 1988, especially when it came to music labels. Factory was on its arse. The Smiths weren't around. The only thing that had a future was all that acid house stuff, but it wasn't as if there was a real outlet for that sort of thing. It's no wonder my office was swamped with blokes holding cassettes.

People knock Pete Waterman for being a manipulator and a proponent of tacky music. But he's a good worker. All those years digging graves have held him in good stead. When he set his office up in Manchester a couple of years later he gave people a chance, and not in a Simon Cowell way. He never made enthusiastic kids feel worthless in the way that Cowell does. The simple fact was that Manchester needed him at the time. They'd all have a laugh at him, at his music, at his clothes, but he knew what he was doing.

He was always alright with me. In 1996 I worked on a single with him and these two lads called Dose – the single was called 'Plug Myself In'. I couldn't come up with a hook line for the song. So they brought in eight people to work one out, four women from London and four lickarses from Manchester, plus these two lads from Dose. It wasn't the best of times for me. I was drinking a lot and I didn't have much money. One minute they're all my best friends, having a drink and all that; and then they're complaining to Waterman, saying, 'He won't do this and he won't do that!' We all had a meeting in this big room, Final Solution style. Wartime *Pop Idol*. They wanted to say,

'Sing this,' and then discuss what we'd just heard. I wasn't having any of it. Waterman just said, 'What's the problem? Do you know who you're talking to? If you fucking carry on like this you're fired, because you're talking to Mark E. Smith. Whatever he wants to do he can do. However much he wants, give it to him.'

The single went nowhere of course, but I respected him for that.

Cog Sinister just ran its course. It was okay releasing Fall stuff but the minute I took a gamble on new acts that's when it got tricky. They didn't sell. If I'd stuck to my own LPs it would have been a different story. But at least I never let it spiral out of control like Factory. People got paid and I tried to help a few mates out. Everybody knew where they stood. I don't have any regrets about doing it. It was non-stop in the end though. I'd be writing and touring and trying to concentrate on Cog all at the same time. That's why we had to use Fontana as a vanity label.

People ask me why I don't set another label up. But it's not something that interests me at the moment. You need the right people when you're embarking on projects like that. And I'm not talking about people who know their music or how to balance accounts, but people with scruples, because eventually there'll come a time when things either hit the wall or go stellar. Either way, you've got nervous breakdowns in the offing.

And I have enough of that with the group and the other things that have a tendency to threaten your sanity.

He said he'd have a uniform for me by the end of the week; if not, the week after. G.B. doesn't like us to work in our normal day-to-day clothes, but with the way things are, with the chaos and all, they've not much choice . . .

14. A Man Alone

It sounds crackers now, but I moved to Edinburgh in 1989 because, firstly, I needed to get away from Brix. Also, I didn't like Manchester at the time. It was all turning very hippy-fied. And I wasn't getting on with the group.

It was an impulsive thing; and the only place I'd been to that I actually liked was Edinburgh. Not the people, just the way it looked.

I was in one of those periods when it was time for a change. I just thought to myself, 'Well, you're not too badly off – you're in a job that allows you to work anywhere you want. So why stay here?' And I scooted.

I divorced Brix – she went to London and I went to Edinburgh.

I'd never lived on my tod before in my life. It's ridiculous really: thirty years old and never lived alone. I just needed time, not necessarily to get myself together but to get *things* together. It was good for me. I just packed a few clothes and got a mate of mine to drive me to the train station.

At first, it was quite worrying. I moved to Leith, and it's a mixture of working-class and upper-class people there. I was the only Englishman around. Thankfully, it turned out great. I walked into a pub and they liked me. They didn't like the English but they liked me. So I made friends very easily, mostly with people who didn't know who I was. I liked the way they weren't your mates because of who you were – they were just your pals. I used to go on the piss with doctors and coppers and acid heads and all sorts. The problem was, I wasn't getting much writing done.

I had an advance from Polygram, the record label. I wasn't living it up or anything. I spent a lot of time in these small specialized science and law libraries. They were the perfect places to go and kill a few hours before you had a drink. I'd peruse all these great psychiatric reports and law files. I spent a lot of time in there, just reading bits and pieces from these strange papers. It was like a second education in a way. I'd never read anything quite like that before. And, more importantly, it was all free. Anybody was allowed in there. It's not closed off like it is here, where only a doctor knows what a doctor does. You could have a cig in some of them as well. Some fellows used to bring hip flasks in; you'd see them nipping away while reading about nineteenth-century law. It was very civilized. That's how it should be in England. Go into a library round here and you've got a load of repressed stormtroopers gawking at you. It's no wonder kids don't read as much as they used to.

I'd go for walks as well, take in a few sights. Edinburgh has a lot of great buildings – truly spectacular monuments. And the place itself has a good feel to it. I couldn't have picked a better environment.

At night I'd go out and have a drink with my new pals. But the more I think about it, the more I remember it as a heavy scene; not too dissimilar to *Trainspotting*. I still have a few mates there. But they do tend to live very fast in Leith. People my age are virtually retired with six kids now; grandfathers at forty. I'm talking about men who were spiking it up in their twenties when I was with them – doing everything.

I know a lot of people who were unhappy with *Trainspotting*. They didn't like the way that whole scene was depicted. It's true that Welsh was very much a fringe player. He didn't go as far as a lot of others, and so of course they think he's a bit of a stool pigeon. I liked it, though. I was one of the first people to read it. I recommended it to a lot of my mates. The simple fact is you don't have to be a complete fuck-up to write about being a fuck-up. I think they've got it wrong there. You'd have to be quite stupid to think otherwise; and there's not that much difference between jacking up for three months and jacking up for a year or however long. It's not as if he wrote about it in a *Guardian* way. He didn't slum it for a few months and then chivvy on back to Notting Hill. I think he nailed it well. He's a good writer, just a shame he didn't put us on the soundtrack to *Trainspotting* – I needed a few quid at the time!

Wintertime was good there as well. They don't celebrate Christmas like they do in England. I remember being alone in my flat and just wandering to the pub every day and the atmosphere was nothing like it is in England – none of that straining for a good time. It seemed less commercial there as well. It was great. But the big thing in Scotland is hogmanay – that's a free for all. And it lasts for days. Fantastic – free drinks, whisky.

Christmas is a weird time to be in England, especially where I live. People get more emotional as the years go by; people I haven't heard from in months ring me up all sad and wistful. It's like a confession, like they're conferring a darkness upon themselves and I'm their sounding board. There was none of that in Edinburgh. It was more like the last days of Rome – strangers coming up to you with a half a bottle of whisky in a pint glass.

'Here you go, sonny!'

I think that's where the problems started. I got a real taste for it. There's nothing quite like being drunk on whisky. Things can get mental on that stuff; and things did get mental years later; but while in Edinburgh I handled it well. I was happy to be out of Manchester. I couldn't have stuck around and witnessed all that Madchester bollocks. I thought it was all very childish really; cynical and childish and empty. I don't know what I would have done if I'd been around then.

Part of me wishes I'd stayed in Leith. The flat I had was fantastic; this beautiful Victorian house with a big luxurious couch and all this classic art on the walls. Cobble stone; before all that sort of thing became trendy. I see that area quite a lot on property programmes. It'd cost you about half a million quid now. Typical me; I gave it up. I could have just signed the lease – it was only a year and a half lease and I was paying twenty-five quid a week all in – electric, gas, etc.

I came back for a number of reasons, one of which was that it was too nice there. This is another thing with me. Sometimes things can be too good. I am like that. People call it self-destructive. You can become too comfortable; and I do care about my writing. It's alright getting up when you want and making a few phone calls when you want, going to a few museums, a few clubs; but all the time you're finding excuses not to write.

My dad died in 1989 as well. It was a bad period. All the males in the family started dropping off, too. I'd have to come back every month or so: go back to Edinburgh after six weeks and Uncle Jimmy's dead; a month later my grandad's dead; a month after that Uncle Ernie's dead. They all just dropped off the perch. Quite weird, really. In the space of about six to nine months I was going through a divorce and most of the male members of my family had died. After nearly a year in Edinburgh I was the only male in the family. I went from being Mark the daft fellow who never goes on *Top of the Pops* to being something entirely different. They were all bastions of the family. They left a big hole.

All that remained was me, Uncle Norman and about twenty women. It's quite common, that. Salford has one of the worst death rates for middle-aged males; higher than parts of the Third World.

Looking back, I do remember having a feeling that I had to return to Manchester. It wasn't as if I'd been hiding or that I was frightened. Manchester had been my home for a long time; an unhealthy amount of time almost.

★

To be honest, I'm trying to get back to my Edinburgh regime today – eating three square meals a day of good food. And good fresh air helps a lot as well. Rather than moping around Prestwich, where you're lucky to get a packet of bacon.

The one thing I do regret is not buying that flat. It killed me financially. I'm hopeless with things like that. Before I ·went, I had all these pension plans. But I let it all go to pot. Just thought – fuck it!

Me and Brix were shelling out two hundred quid a month for health insurance and Bupa and a pension plan. Things were quite straight in that respect. But the longer I spent in Edinburgh the more broke I became.

I suppose I ought to be glad I didn't continue with all that shit anyway. A lot of people around the ages of fifty and fifty-five who invested in things like that can't get their money back now. Not long after I couldn't afford to invest any more, Robert Maxwell died and all that pension corruption business became public news. I knew people in the music business who were paying out £600 a month for pension plans and all those companies have collapsed. I do remember feeling guilty about not keeping up the payments, though.

You've got to make your mind up – pay the group a decent wage, pay your divorce or your pension plan; looked at like that it's not that important. But in those days financial advisers would come round to your house wanting to know why you'd fallen behind; they even tried to come up to Edinburgh.

A lot of people went solo because of that pension business. People were telling me to do likewise, saying, 'Why shell your money out on the band when you can put it in a pension plan? You're like a footballer, you'll be fucked up when you're thirty-five – save your money.'

But I thought it was more important to pay the group – not that they appreciated it. I always paid handsome wages, which backfired. I was very socialistic. Everybody got paid the same. It's not a bad job at all. But I was working with lower-middle-class people who think you're a bit stupid. They all think you're an idiot. Maybe it's because I'm not a musician – they don't think I understand their 'creative angst'.

They say things like, 'Why aren't we like U2? Why aren't *we* at the top of the album charts?'

After I've just paid them more than what those bands were receiving! But my attitude was, it's better to do that in order to remain independent.

They couldn't understand why they weren't playing stadiums, failing to realize the fact that they're doing something they want to do and earning the same money as fucking Bono. I had the same thing with Ben and Steve. I'd have to keep saying to them, 'You're getting the same money as Franz Ferdinand but you don't have to make a fool of yourself every five minutes on TV. You can record what you want. It doesn't have to be a hit. Stop whining!'

I think they get to a stage where they think they're carrying me – that I'm holding *them* back just for the stubborn hell of it.

A lot of people think I'm an idiot because I keep paying these people. But I don't see it like that. Where would I be now if I didn't continue to do that? In a nice big house in Cheshire on my tod! Not doing anything. Looking forward to the gardener coming around. Popping down to the nice local pub. What would I do? I would have been dead at forty-five, that's what.

Despite not getting a lot of writing done in Edinburgh, the time I spent there resulted in *Extricate* (1990), which is still a well-liked album. A lot of good writing originates from periods like that, when you don't force it too much. Even the critics liked it. But I think they read too much into it. Every question they asked me would be like, 'This single here – this is about Brix, isn't it?'

It's never that clear-cut. Even 'Bill is Dead' – which everybody assumed was about my dad and his mate Bill – began as a piss-take of The Smiths. Only later did it become something a little more personal.

There's not a bad track on it, if you ask me. I'm very proud of that LP. Stuff like 'Popcorn Double Feature', that's a cover of a Searchers track. I've always been a big fan of The Searchers. Everybody goes on about The Beatles, but The Searchers were the main Merseybeat band for me. They were brilliant songwriters, very underrated. That whole scene's very underrated. Music buffs harp on about the *Nuggets* groups and 60s American garage music – which is all very good – but there was also a lot of great music originating from Liverpool at the time. I think that's why The La's were the only group I liked around '89. The Happy Mondays and The Stone Roses were alright, but they were never as good as The La's. Lee Mavers was brilliant; they were very similar to The Searchers in a soulful way.

As I say, I'm very proud of *Extricate*. Like with *Hex* before it and *The Real New Fall LP* after, I think I proved something there. It does bring the best out of me when I'm forced into a corner. I don't wilt like other people. I'm used to being up against it. Being brought up the way I was helps.

If I wasn't who I am, I wouldn't stand a fucking chance nowadays. I'm trouble. They'd rather have somebody straight-weird like Ian Brown or Russell Brand; a fellow who can be reined in, given enough coercing. They don't want anybody like me. They don't want the honest stuff – somebody saying I don't want that, I don't want anything to do with that. But I'm incapable of toeing the line. If something is clearly wrong or third-rate I'm not willing to let it go. I get that from my dad. He had a good head for correcting mistakes while remaining a decent bloke.

Just before he died he asked me if he'd ever done me wrong. He never gave me any problems. He was great. The older I get, the more I remember things he used to say to me, things like, 'If you're feeling too sexy have a glass of water and a run round the backyard.' That's brilliant. I'll always appreciate what he did for me and my sisters and my mam.

15. Hard as Nails

I am one of the 3 per cent who was made to take speed. It helps me sleep. It's not a big problem for me, but I can always tell when people are writing on drugs. On speed it's all nonsense.

I remember Nick Cave when he used to write on heroin, he'd show me his lyrics. I'd be like, 'Nick, what you doing?' From The Birthday Party to this – lyrics like, 'Ohh, I went to the canal, fell in the lake.' That's what heroin's like, you think you're really good. I did it once at a party in Manchester in the mid 80s, just to be sociable. I started writing, thinking this is the greatest thing ever written. Then I fell asleep. I woke up some time the day after, thinking I'd written the masterpiece of all masterpieces. I was convinced I'd written a short story, a novel, and an LP all in one. I felt like shit, told myself I'm not taking that again, but at least I'd got this work of genius.

And then I started reading it, or trying to read it; this four-page epic. It was a mess. I'd fallen asleep on the fifth page. I didn't even know what it was, whether it was a song or a story.

It fools you, proper heroin. It's quite scary. You can see it with the likes of Pete Doherty. He thinks he's created something that isn't there. It plays the worst of all tricks on you. Never again; the first and last time – I hated the stuff. Why bother? You'll be like that anyway when you're ninety and dying.

I get classed with the Beat writers sometimes, in that people think I'm under the influence when I write; which isn't always the case.

There's a rumour with William Burroughs, though, that he didn't take as much as he cracked on he did; that a lot of it was an image thing: the experimenter. He was a clever man in that respect.

Contrary to what a lot of critics think, I've never been influenced by him. I'm not such a big fan of his work. In fact, I don't particularly like *Naked Lunch*. It's almost unreadable, if you ask me. *Cities of the Red Night* is much better. But most of his stuff is boring, almost as if he's doing it for the money in order to go and get some more little boys in Tangiers or wherever. I think Ginsberg was the more interesting writer. He was the one who took all the drugs as well. His lines are clearer, less dense. He doesn't hide as much as Burroughs.

But it's not really about the drink and drugs, is it? To some people it is; to some people that's it – if you take drugs or you have a pint or two, then they're not going to go any further with you. But to me they're missing the point; which is, if you are going to take shit, then it's essential that it doesn't get in the way of what you're doing, that you handle it as best you can. I get the feeling with Doherty and a lot of young lads nowadays that they're acting the rock star without delivering the goods. It's empty success, in other words. It's fine when they're shooting up or they're arm in arm with supermodels, but sit them down and ask them to record an album and they're fucking straight off to rehab. They get sloppy too quickly.

It used to be the case that models attached themselves to real rock stars – Anita Pallenberg and Marianne Faithfull with The Stones in the 60s, for instance; but that's not the case nowadays. That says it all for me. Any berk with a scruffy hair-do and a couple of songs can find an outlet and hero-worship like that nowadays.

What gets me is when I get daft promoters like Alan Wise saying, 'Don't give Mark the whisky before he goes on.' It's written into the contract – 'Do not give Mark whisky before he goes on stage.' I'd rather have it upfront. Most of the people saying things like that are obviously zipped out of their brains themselves.

I've known about drugs since I was fourteen, and I can tell when somebody's not all there, when their eyes are telling me they've done too much chokey. If I was a copper I'd lock them up straight away. But I'm too well mannered to say that. What's more, I can see if they've had eight cups of coffee as well, which is not good for you. I miss all those fellows, all my old Irish mates, in that respect. If somebody said to them, 'Have you been drinking, sir?' they'd be like 'Yes, I fucking have, and I want some more – what's it got to do with you?' But you can't say that any more – you'd get thrown off a plane for a start.

To a certain extent I understand where they're coming from. I did happen to lose it a bit when I was drinking too much whisky in the mid 90s, but I checked myself. I knew I had to curb it. And I did. I stand by Whyte and Mackay though, it's a lovely drink.

The worst thing I could do now is completely stop. You look at the amount of people who have died because they've just stopped drinking or doing whatever. The list is endless. The thing with me is, I don't get hangovers. I've never been bothered by them. Red wine gets to me; it makes me very violent. I think it's bad for you. Women who are into red wine are always manic-depressives.

The only hangovers I've ever had were off ecstasy. It's not nice. It's like going to hospital and being drugged up when you've had an accident. Very much like when I broke my leg. You're drying your brain up with that stuff, it's like a sponge. You feel sort of high, you go home, but in the morning it's as if you've eaten a lot of dust.

I remember in the Hacienda days when you couldn't get any drink or speed – they'd all be dancing around and touching you. What the fuck is all this about? I don't need to feel like this.

I can feel like this in hospital. It's like a gross antidepressant mixed with speed. They all want to love everybody.

All of a sudden you've turned into a sex maniac. Mates of mine from Salford who used to take the piss out of me for being in The Fall suddenly start gushing, 'I've always liked you, Mark.' It's terrible, they start getting eloquent about plastering or roofing. I preferred it when they used to threaten me. But I don't trust any artificial drugs. A friend of a friend once told me how they made it. It was very fishy the way it was invented. The aim was to get American middle-class kids off the street. So some scientist came up with this mixture of coke, speed, pot and acid; the chemical equivalent. Perfect. Work all week, do what you want, and take it at the weekend. State control: Brave New World.

I'm not a big fan of pot, either. It cuts people off from their feelings, like Prozac. You've got to come out some time.

At least you know where you are with booze. You drink two bottles of whisky and wake up in the morning, you know you've done something wrong, you know you won't be doing that again. But experience tells you it'll lift soon. And with liquor, if you drink any more you'll be dead. You can't move. But with E you start seeing chickens on the road – I know I was.

It's always been the same with my drinking. It annoys me when fellows go on about it, sitting there with a pint telling me what I should and shouldn't be doing. It's more about them than it is about me. They usually drink as much as I do, if not more. The difference is they work at a completely different job. I don't have to be up at a certain time every day. It's jealousy, in a way. I find it amusing when they bang on about how much they eat, how healthy they are – 'I eat four meals a day, me.' And I'm like, 'Yeah, and look where it's got you.' They fail to realize that 99.9 per cent of people with a healthy diet will eventually die.

It's a strange phenomenon that, people discussing their lunches. Kids used to do that at school. But now I'll get on the bus, or I'll be sat in the pub, and all I can hear is people discussing the contents of their guts or the meal that they've got in their heads: 'I had some nice tomato sauce last night with chips.'

I don't know why they're telling you this. It's the same when you ring people up and ask them how they're doing and they say something like, 'I'm okay, Mark. I've just had a curry. I wish I didn't have this headache, though. I've not been feeling too good lately.'

You're not supposed to react like that. You're supposed to say, 'Yeah, I'm alright. How are you? Now what do you want?'

But I really can't stand it when blokes feel the need to comment on your drinking habits. It's rampant, all that malarkey: New Labour trying to keep people alive for ever. I don't see them berating the royals or their backbenchers about having a cig or a large gin at 3 o'clock in the afternoon. If you put it in the context of the current climate, having a few pints and a Benson after work is hardly the worst crime on earth. It's the same when you go to the doctor. I don't know what it is with them and smokers. It's common knowledge that some doctors are the worst degenerates in existence. They've been on everything in their time. But as soon as you tell them you've got a bad back or a gammy leg, their first question is, 'Well, are you a smoker?' What the fuck does that have to do with it?

People are infected by all this guff. You can tell them anything. They'll eat anything that claims to stop them burping or 'may' prolong their lives by a few seconds. Red meat and liquids – that's all you need.

I'm annoyed by the lack of smoking on TV as well. It's terrible. It's funny seeing old interviewers lighting up, the likes of Russell Harty pulling on a Three Castles or a State Express or a Churchman Full Strength or a Passing Cloud. I think it's a shame that we don't get to see this any more. We should have more ashtrays on morning TV and presenters wheezing.

Alan Wise got the shock of his life. He finished a tour with us a few years ago and afterwards he said, 'I'm glad to get rid of you lot, drinking whisky all the time. Bastards, The Fall. Ignorant north Mancunians. I'm going on tour with Jerry Lee Lewis and Chuck Berry: a nice tour.' Totally ignorant. Totally Mancunian. It's totally isolated, Manchester.

He goes, 'It'll be good to get on the road with two old men like Chuck and Jerry.'

I said, 'Fucking hell, dream on, mate!'

Jerry just locked himself in his dressing room every night, then kicked the shit out of his piano. He only played a short set, then kicked the stool over and fucked off back to his dressing room.

He wouldn't talk to Chuck Berry, hated him. All the Chuck Berry fans, all the John Lennon scouser fans, were dressed up in their 50s gear. Jerry just stared them out; he didn't even let on to his group.

What a great show – brilliant! I saw it in Manchester. I was standing up, shouting, 'Jerry, Jerry!' This is just after I'd fucked my leg up in Newcastle. The funny thing was I went to see it with Shaun Bainey, our manager at the time, and a mate of mine, James Fennings, who DJs for us. Both of them were freaking out – they couldn't handle it. I loved it. Morrissey turned up as well, waiting around in his best suit backstage to see Chuck – his best mate. I left after Jerry had done his thing. My work was done.

On the third day of the tour Wisey finally mustered up the courage to go and ask Jerry what he'd like. Jerry wouldn't talk to him. He thought he looked like a junkie. So Wisey's like, 'You didn't tell me they were like this. Nico wasn't like this. New Order are not like this.'

I said, 'I told you, it's The Killer, man!' He hadn't a clue who he was dealing with, hadn't even bothered to read up on them. Because if you're a promoter in Manchester most of the time all you're doing is driving Barney out of New Order to the guitar shop for some new strings. That's what it's like in Manchester. They live in a fantasy world. It's not rock and roll.

They expected two old fellows in wheelchairs. Not The Killer with his two limousines – one for his group and one for him.

And not Chuck Berry striding off the plane with his guitar, demanding five thousand quid now or I'm gone . . . He wouldn't play otherwise. Everybody knows that's the way Chuck Berry operates. But they're so Hacienda – Wisey didn't have a clue. 'Oh we'll have to go to the bank first.'

So he walks back to the plane. Damn right. That's what I'd do.

All of a sudden they find five thousand quid. Two minutes later, he gets driven to the nearest Hertz van hire.

'Get me a car now – the best you've got!'

He hires a car and asks them to write out the address of the first show. Promoters just can't do this sort of thing. A child can, but not them – they're incapable of simple things like that; it's the same in America. They can't just write down the itinerary for you – your hotel, the street, first gig, etc. It's beyond them. After fucking around, they finally get him the address. And he blasts off on the wrong side of the road wearing one of his suits. He's already had his clothes sent to the hotel; all his suits. That's rock and roll.

Wisey thought he was dealing with Donovan. He thought he could have a nice little rest, cup of tea. How Manchester is that?

I liked the way everybody started jumping on the Johnny Cash bandwagon as well. If you were a Cash fan in the 70s people thought you were a racist. Nobody admitted to it. He and Elvis were more unfashionable than the so-called dinosaurs like Pink Floyd and Led Zeppelin. That's what Julie Burchill and Tony Parsons thought – they even said it to me, they called it redneck music. It's a different story now he's dead. Suddenly Parsons has been a Cash fan all his life. Nobody gave a fuck about him in the late 70s and 80s and then all of a sudden he's the new dead icon.

I find it horrible the way they've made money out of him, releasing all these maudlin recordings. Give me early Cash any day. People love it, though, all that sentimental shit; they can't be arsed discovering what he was really like. It's a shame that. I'm sure his family aren't too happy about it either.

That film was a disgrace as well. Not that I watched it, I refused to. What's the point? It's the same with all those music biopics. As a fan you might as well just watch the real thing. You can't replicate it. Would you rather see *Walk the fucking Line* with River Phoenix's daft brother or Cash *Live at San Quentin*? It's not as if Hollywood's going to give you all the facts, anyway. It's just some watered-down, sanitized version. It's pointless. It's all about people, Hollywood people mostly, who just want to attach themselves to this type of character; cool by association.

Guys like Cash and Jerry and Link Wray and Iggy Pop even are very special to me. Their art comes from rich experience, you can't fake that authenticity. It can't be manipulated. They just go where instinct tells them, and more often than not it works. I admire that. There's not enough of that around.

It's a thin line but I think the point is not to get what you want or to settle for what you've got, but to understand what it is you want and to go for it; it's in the understanding.

Guide to Manchester

There is a lot business and also a cheerful place.

Kera Ellis said Manchester is a lovely place to live.

In the shopping centres, they are busy.

The streets are olvaring and lovely.

The streets have lots of trouble at night.

My place means a lot to me.

It's a brilliant place to live in – nice culture too, many nice
people like Tony Wilson for instance, or Ding.

Like Fay McGlochin said watching lovely food – belies
description.

As do the Security Staff at the former Fab Caff – one hired
from Cheshire – one hired PE teacher training – the rest
obligatory black and tan ex-convicts from the council who
pretend they like Morrissey.

Going up out of it – you can easily spot it – turning right
they're Red twats like Rob Curtis ready to guide your way
to Chorlton or Didsbury – getting your way out,
organizing yr luggage you will find a mate to help you
whose dad was in the Air-Force-Polish.

Chain-Chelsea-Putty

By now your hands will be changed Chelsea-like putty.

Already, like most Manchester musicians group you will be
crying hysterically

And artistically in a false way. It makes sense for you by

hour, 2 stay in the hills and avoid the enzyme of the
virulent city centres!
Like Noel (that popular dwarf), or Clint – you can go back,
return and scoff your face.
Historically it makes sense for you 2 stay in the hills and
don't experience city centres!

Manchester – my Manchester
I love the place so well.
I also love the people –
Who have a tale to tell.
It's a city you'll never forget.
I'm Pauline – Summat
Some say that M/cr is often cold and cruel
But once you've been here . . .

I'm the History of the World

Please call me:
All
RAKES.

As All is as one,
As all damp on all stone,

I hold the time,
And can Entreat At once,

All Jets and trains, lead panes,
Spin complete.
And real rebellions spawn/complete
Revolutions.

Spawn Follies and Theorem;
Crossword United programmes
Misread Easter. I stand, Put
Butter on Plague-Stile

And I Alter,
Tree Rings so What Are You After
In Historytown
You Won't Find
BEGGAR in East End,
Lice-ridden before nite
Imagining thru hunger a
BREAD tree spinning
In complete revolutions.

I'M THE HISTORY
OF THE WORLD
I'M HISTORY
Yo Cheeky World.

Sufficiently Strenuous
2 deter flirts

Go out little tyke –

Meet at crossroads

Early morning

The sick hills near Buxton

Softly roll

I got to do it

Prefixed about it

Gotta meet Jim with the

                         Roll –

He's a lazy hill-person

Late – and slow as usual

A Ted Hughes human

Semi Mole.

My Top

BUT, the last and final straw. They at first appeared wrong.
   Then it started – first the ash down the back. Modern and
   chic – an Abundance of style.
Rachel-warm and friendly. Busy and bright.
Tune in the tube
day time.

At night, I love my
1 p.m.
THAT WAS MY ROOM.

Words found on a Cassette of 23/01/06

1/ A – Systematic.

2/ Clasp Hands.

3/ Ben plays Clasp Hands.

4/ I Am Mental by Ben.

5/ I Am Mental/Gray Hair.

6/ Typhoon Reggae Police.

7/ TV – Music – End.

8/ A FATS PACE SONG.

16. I'm on the Hard Road Again

I never use hip studios. If I've got the money I always make sure I use the straightest and the best. That's where half of the money has gone. I don't want the studio where The Pet Shop Boys or Morrissey have recorded. I don't need it. I know it's going to be shit.

Even when I was skint after the divorce, I still insisted we use a top-quality studio for *Shift-Work* (1991). In the end we used UB40's recording studio; I'm talking a really good studio here. As well as complaining about us robbing their tea bags, UB40 were saying things like, 'Why aren't The Fall recording where Nick Cave or Sonic Youth record – a real cool joint, with all the facilities, where you can stay over and all that?' I'd rather record with guys who don't know who The Fall are; fellows who've been working with Status Quo, which was the case on *This Nation's Saving Grace*. Quo was their standard. These are guys who won't put up with sloppiness. They don't like The Fall, but they'll do the job. If you're going to play it out of tune, then play it out of tune properly. The idea is you get a group like us in there and everybody's getting a boot up the arse. And it does show in the work. The sound on our LPs is actually a damn sight better than on, say, Oasis LPs. It may have cost a fraction of what they've spent, but it is good, because it's properly engineered.

Recording is another world altogether. You shouldn't do what some groups do, and go with a mate of a mate who's bought his own studio. It's a mistake.

I was very disappointed with the studio in LA where we went to finish *Reformation*, because they were making out it was a proper heavy metal studio and it wasn't. Ben and that lot had done some dismal stuff in Lincolnshire, and the idea was we'd wrap it up in this studio. It was no cheap affair, either. That's another thing that pissed me off. We'd booked a substantial amount of time in this place. The group knew the deal. In truth, they bottomed out of the contract, because we entered that place with a completely different band. Fair play to The Dudes, they did what they could.

The engineer wasn't on the ball, though. He wasn't a bad bloke, he was just having a few domestic problems.

Whether you like them or not, a proper London engineer who's worked with The Stone Roses will tell you you've got to do things again and concentrate. And it works. You can't just bang it out live – it's totally different from a gig.

But in the same respect, I'm not such a fan of albums being re-mastered. It's usually to the detriment of the listener. Once they start fiddling with it, adding tracks and embellishing this and that, it takes the heart out of the thing. It's the same with filmmakers who can't stop fiddling. Having said that, it seemed to work on *Hex*. It unearthed a lot of things, a lot of sounds.

I remember recording 'Mr Pharmacist' at Abbey Road in the mid 80s around the time when CDs were the new thing. The second day I was there I walked up the stairs to the cutting room and I couldn't get in the door due to a stack of mail. I asked one of the producer guys what it all was, and he told me it was complaint mail for The Beatles. The Beatles were one of the first bands to get the whole re-issue treatment, but the fans couldn't listen to it. Years of listening to the original vinyl and then this . . . to them it might as well have been a different band.

People aren't as daft as you think. There were so many of these letters they had to stick them in the back room – they couldn't answer them.

It's the same with Elvis. 'Heartbreak Hotel' on CD is almost a completely different song from on vinyl. You've got forty-odd tracks to monkey around with on CD, and not four – as was the case with the original recording. And you can hear all these nonsense noises. It's flat. Instead of having all the sounds at the front, like they did with the original, they've flattened it out across forty-odd tracks; one here, one there.

What a lot of people don't realize is that you've got these total strangers in the cutting room fiddling around – that's what they mean by re-mastered. You might as well ask a fellow in the pub to do it, at least he'll have some knowledge of the music he's butchering. It'd probably work out better that way. It's not as if the people working on the re-mastering give a shit about the acts – to them it's just a new way to waste time, and the record companies know full well that they'll wangle a bit more dough out of it. It's just dolling up the dead. Instead of using their energy to promote the living they'd rather go down the Burke and Hare path. They always make a big thing out of it as well: the re-mastered version. It's just another cynical record company trick. How many versions of *Sgt Pepper* can one man own? The daft thing is that people do buy that shit. They must have rocks in their head. It's a racket. We're living in a re-issue world, filching from the past like magpies with a Tardis. I used to take tape recordings of the original vinyl on tour with me. Record them in the kitchen on to tape. You get a bit of fuzz on it, but it sounds better than the CD. Tapes and vinyl are very underrated. It's like the difference between reading a book and reading something on a computer.

The Infotainment Scan (1993) was all about regressive idealism. You can't live in the past like that. It's a lot more dangerous than you think. Kids growing up hearing their mams and dads talk about how great 1976 and 1981 were – it's bullshit. There have never been any great years. You get the odd moment here and there, but never a clean year of wonder.

It died down a little after *Infotainment*, but then Oasis and Blur started name-checking The Beatles and The Small Faces and it returned like a wave of sickness you thought you'd seen the back of. And then all of a sudden you've got those ridiculous list programmes – *One Hundred Great Horror Films* and whathavya.

On the other hand, I can't stand these lads thickening up their accents and singing about shit kisses and cigs and chip shops, this affected realism – it's not that far removed from George Formby.

People have a go at things like *Coronation Street* for adopting a similar broad northernness, but if you watch it and listen to it closely its use of language is quite cutting edge. The scriptwriters have a good ear for any new phrases that are circling Manchester.

In the mid 90s I used to drink in a pub called The Grapes near Granada's studios – Vera Duckworth (Elizabeth Dawn) owns it now. It's a good pub. You get a few cast members and scriptwriters in there. I'd have a couple of pints with Simon Gregson, who plays Steve McDonald – nice bloke. And there'd be scriptwriters dotted around, scribbling. It doesn't always work. Sometimes the dialogue's very clunky, as if the writers have been too keen to use new phrases, but when it does work it's far superior to a lot of things out there.

You're not progressing if it's just about sounding exactly like where you're from. There's got to be more to it than that. I get sent a lot of CDs that suffer from this. They think because I'm proud of where I'm from and don't hide my accent that that's all it's about. I must admit I don't listen to new CDs as much as I used to, for this reason. I know what I'm in for. Most of the time it'll be some bloke with a broad accent telling me about his night out or what it's like to be skint, with some interesting guitar or electronic noise behind him. It's not bad. I'm not one to have a go at people for doing it. I just think it's limited.

The main problem with it is its lack of humour. I've always found The Fall humorous. I'm surprised when people don't get that side of us. It's glaringly obvious to me. I'm not one for wallowing in grimness like a lot of other groups are. There's money to be made out of doing that. You only have to listen to the likes of Coldplay. They only have one tone or mood. They can't step it up. But that's not been The Fall's way.

A lot of what we did in the 90s has been overlooked because of the Mad Mark side of things. I went from being a provocative drunk to being public enemy number one. I was drinking a lot of whisky at the time – too much, probably. But I still think the work stands for itself. Even *The Light User Syndrome* (1996), which is often dismissed as a whisky-rash of an album, has its moments. I still hear people talking about 'Cheetham Hill'; and the likes of Primal Scream just robbed the whole sound of that album in the 90s.

The ironic thing was that you had the accepted rebels like Bobby Gillespie and Shaun Ryder and Liam Gallagher – who were all fawned upon in one way or another; and then you had me!

I've never played the game like they have. The Happy Mondays and Oasis would do anything. The *NME* would say, 'We're having a party for the staff in London,' and there'd be about 150 people and their mates, public not allowed. The Happy Mondays would come down and play. I'd never do that. I'm talking about playing private parties for record executives at Creation Records, which Oasis did. What's more, Creation used to ring me up and say, 'We know you haven't got a label, and we really want to sign you if you do this: if you come down and play this informal party for the Creation staff and Alan McGee.'

And I'm like, 'If you're a Fall fan, as you say you are, why do I have to play a party?'

'Oh, it'd be in your interests, Mark.'

The Mondays did loads of that shit, and New Order did as

well. You've got to do it. That's what I've had to deal with for years. Sorry, I'm not singing for some fat nobody – fuck that!

And then all of a sudden I got a very bad reputation for only playing for half an hour, for just shouting and then walking off. I don't see why you can't do it. But in the mid 90s we couldn't get shows because of it. It was alright for The Jesus and Mary Chain – it was hip when they did that. But when I did it we got the opposite reaction. And then we had a reputation for not turning up on time and me being abusive – which was a pack of rumours. That's why we now pride ourselves on being on time and playing for the exact limit. Just to see their faces.

It was any excuse for them not to pay you. Countless times we didn't get paid in the 90s; couldn't even get booked. It was all over the place. What can you do?

Looking back, I should never have got Trevor Long in to manage us. He brought about my bankruptcy. I met him just after we'd done *Kurious, Oranj* (1988). He'd worked with Dexys Midnight Runners, and he seemed like he knew what he was up to, seemed competent.

He was a pro alright.

At the time, I couldn't really put my finger on it. It was so strange the way our money kept going up and down. The problem stemmed from the fact I've always insisted on paying people equal wages. I wanted to take control of most things. I never wanted musicians to worry about money. If you're going to do it, then centre it.

I took him to court in the end in 1994.

My argument to the prosecution was that his job was to go and *garner* some money. But he had this really good barrister who said, 'Mr Smith, who's a pop singer, says he was supposed to *garner* – whatever that means.' Everybody knows what that means. The judge just laughed. It was like *The Prisoner*: everybody just laughing in my face And then they threw out the evidence because I quoted a figure of £1,200 when the actual figure was £1,215.

It couldn't have worked out any worse.

There was a microphone in front of me that I thought I was talking into, but it wasn't even plugged in. I must have looked like a right idiot – I didn't notice it until the third day.

The money I could have got from the whole case would have settled all the tax problems.

Then something weird happened. The Curse of The Fall: it doesn't happen in ones, it comes in twos and threes. My accountant, who'd been brilliant for years, joined forces with an Asian company that turned out to be corrupt, although of course he didn't know that. They initiated the bankruptcy. The minute he hooked up with them they started charging me a ridiculous amount of money for consultations. And it was at a time when that sort of money just wasn't coming in. And so after three or four months he had to petition me for bankruptcy. I'd only been working with them theoretically for three or four months. Everything had been okay before they came on the scene.

I had some very low days. I was drinking a lot, a real lot. Going to meet accountants and having band meetings pissed out of my head wasn't the best idea. But what was I supposed to do? I was down. Bad reviews kept piling in about how drunk I was. It all came at once. In a way, I let it happen.

You have to remember, sometimes, people aren't like you. I'm not saying I'm special; only that a lot of people aren't built like me. And you can see why.

It taught me a lesson. You find out who your friends are virtually within a couple of weeks. Video directors who once phoned up for a chat – no more. Even the group got a bit funny.

Now it wasn't, 'How are you, Mark?', more, 'How's the group going to survive? What about us?'

If you're in a group, suddenly these happy mams and dads are at your throat. They've just thrown a big party for the birth of their new kid – they've bought all the presents. Three months later they haven't been paid for a few weeks, and they're at you. What a fucking shame! I was on the dole for years – I didn't get that amount of money. So my attitude was – if you don't like it, get lost.

I wasn't going to sign on the dole again.

The only people who stood by me were my mam – it even got to a stage where I was going round to her house to borrow tins of soup – and my sisters and a few old mates. It goes back to being in gangs as a kid. You stick together. I remember one instance when I was broke. I was sat in a pub in Prestwich village with an old mate of mine, Sean; sat nursing a pint, as you do when you're skint. And I just came out and told him, said, 'I'm broke, Sean. I can't buy you a pint back.'

'I thought you were doing alright?'

'Well, I'm not.'

That's another thing: you're still in the papers but you've got nothing.

And he just went, 'Sit there, Mark,' and fucked off. I thought – here's another one. And then he came back: 'Here, brother – twenty quid.'

JR was another one who stood by me. He's a mate of mine from Prestwich. He was great. He used to come round and knock on my door and say, 'I know you're living on toast. Come on – curry!' And he'd take me for a drink and a curry. He saw the funny side to it all. I appreciate that.

It's hard to write through those periods. It's so much easier to not write. It's alright when you start out and you have no money, that's just part of the game. But it got really bad. Just before I went bankrupt I started hallucinating figures. People would be ringing me up about shows and I wouldn't even be listening. I was hallucinating figures. I remember walking around and all the nice trees had numbers on them. It was worse than LSD. It's amazing I wrote anything in that period. Not eating, and seeing things like that . . .

Then all the bills started coming in. The rehearsal rooms you haven't paid for . . . suddenly they're on at you for eight hundred quid.

It's true what they say about poverty-stricken people in this country. You end up paying more money out than you would do if you were just getting by. For everything; electric, gas, the lot.

I can laugh now, but the minute I went bankrupt I got a bill off the people who were supposed to be defending me. It doesn't happen anywhere else in the world. The legal firm in Manchester who were supposed to be defending me charged me £1,110. They kept ringing up. And I'm like, 'I hate to state the obvious, but I've just gone bankrupt.'

'Oh well, it's none of our business, Mr Smith.' Their tone of voice had changed somewhat.

It's the only place in the world where you lose the case and have to pay the costs.

And then I'd go to the bank. You're trying to explain your situation to them. I can understand it with the tax people, they're not as cutthroat in that respect. They will assess your situation. But not the banks.

I put about a quarter of a million quid through Natwest in about eight or nine years. Then it all went down. They wouldn't even give me an overdraft. It's not like now; the boom period where you can walk in and get a hundred grand for your house. They just said to me, 'You're twenty-eight and you've got no money. You did have money but you gave it all away to your employees.' That was their attitude. 'You can't handle your own finances – why should we give you an overdraft?' They were totally ignoring the fact I'd put a load of dosh in their bank over the previous eight years; dosh that they'd invested. That was all forgotten about.

You can imagine the worry that people with kids and a house have when they have to experience that shit.

I could easily have jacked it all in at that stage. But there's a part of me that's very defiant. I wouldn't have been able to look myself in the mirror if I'd quit. The Fall has always been there for me like that; in a mad way that was all I had.

And then . . .

I'm just glad of the graft. It's not as if I'm actually taking them off the street myself; not as if it's me doing the things they say they do; and you've got to admit, they've been asking for it. I can remember a time when they thought they owned the night . . .

17. The March of the Gormless Bastards

It was doomed from the start.

First American tour in four years, 1998, and it's the same old story: we fly from Manchester to New York and there are two seats empty. Out of five people we're two short. It was the usual palaver, the plane had to wait for an hour or so, and there's just me, Steve Hanley, the bass player, and Julia Nagle, the keyboardist.

I should have known then, it goes back to chokey and amphetamines. They – Karl Burns, the drummer, and Tommy Crooks, the guitarist – hadn't the bottle to get on a plane, because they'd run out of drugs.

So I said to Hanley, 'It doesn't matter, we'll just go without them, do it as a trio.' That's how bad things were.

We got to America, and then I had a heated argument with Julia about sharing a room and we knocked each other about. Hotel security came in with this medic, this Vietnam vet, and they're all going, 'Prosecute her, prosecute her.' Then JR, a mate of mine, turned up at the hotel from out of nowhere – like Jesus. He was on his way to meet some mates in Florida.

But I refused to prosecute. What I think it is, with people who travel like that, those that have never been over the Atlantic, so to speak – they all go a bit funny. We were thrown out of the hotel, JR got us another one and the two idiots – Burns and Crooks – arrive, meaning I play the first three gigs with a black eye.

It turns out they had it all planned for this group of theirs – The Ark – Mark without the M. They'd already booked some studio time in Rochdale that happened to coincide with the tour.

It's strange what this business does to people. Because what they're seeing in New York is people are all over me and they're not over them, so they think well, if he can do it we can do it too.

I remember watching them in a sandwich shop, the three of them, all kissing and hugging each other. I've got a black eye, my only friend is JR and I'm stood with a Chinese fellow and they think you're so daft. I thought, there's something up here, like why are they staying in their hotel rooms all the time? It came out two weeks later. They're on 53rd and 3rd in New York and you've got an American tour coming up and you spend three days in your hotel room, and I'm saying to them, 'Why don't you go out into New York?'

'Well, we're trying to get tight for the gigs,' they say; when, in fact, they weren't, they were working on material for The Ark. People have said I spoil members too much. Split everything to a reasonable point. It's a cack-handed old commie attitude. But the result of that, when everybody gets the same, is that they all think they've got the same power. Fifty per cent of musicians are deceitful, that's what I've found. This is why people go solo. To me they're straights, but not in the right way. They crack on they're artists yet live in a semi-world between the working life and the artistic life – and can't work out which one is real. A lot of circuit groups seem like that. They just want to go home. They want everything comfy: a two-hour sex/craft thing then back in front of the mirror in their bedroom, or in front of a nice roaring fire.

Funnily enough, the morning of the show at Brownie's, I felt I had to meet the group. This is an instance where being psychic isn't all it's cut out to be; you feel it and know it but it's not actually much help. As an old woman said to me once, 'What good is knowing the bus will be a half-hour late?'

Anyway, Das Gruppe, as they appeared to me with their Time-Life books on the Third Reich all over the bus, didn't say a thing about The Ark.

It was supposed to be our penultimate Yank gig, but of course we had an onstage disagreement. They all started throwing punches. But I gave them a few left hooks back. They got worse than they gave me. But that's not nice either, being hit on stage. So I got carried out of the venue by well-meaning security. The crowd are going crazy, they had to be held back. They wanted to rip the band to bits.

Back at the hotel I'm kicking at their doors, shouting, 'Come out, cowards, what's going on?' Of course they didn't.

What I didn't know was that it's an offence to do that, to start shouting, because of the fire regulations. I understand it now.

Julia's no fucking help. So, back in my room, I'm having a cigarette, and I just put it out on her trainer and went to sleep. Next, I've been reported by them and her, and handcuffed and put in jail by a copper who came into the room early in the morning. I'm knackered from all this palaver and she's acting like Princess Diana with the police officer, telling him how much she likes his accent. And they're asking me what happened, and I'm saying, 'I didn't do anything to her, I dimped out a cigarette on her trainer.' She's still jet-lagged and they think she's being abused by a guy who's half dressed, soaking in his anger.

Daft Julia thinks she's talking to English coppers. So when they say to her, 'Does he shout a lot, does he drink a lot?', being from Stockport she doesn't realize that it's a criminal offence in America. She's the sort who'd have bloody advisers over when her husband didn't collect the kids every weekend. She thinks it's that sort of thing – the Cheshire advisory service; failing to realize that these are hard-boiled cops. And they go, 'Is he shouting at his fellow workmates?' And of course they've all said, 'Yeah, he is,' because they've all got their flights booked. She thinks I'm going to go down to the cop shop and get a fine for ten quid or something, not realizing you get rammed in the tombs with a load of murderers.

But, as we were due to play a second night there, the copper said to me, 'If you can prove this, I'll let you go.' They can do that in New York, take you to a show and bring you back. Not to let the people down. But at this point the band were already on the plane. I even asked Hanley to stay, but he was acting like a dinner lady, worried about getting back to Karl and Tommy.

The best thing about it was I got arrested the same day as George Michael. Because on MTV at 6 a.m. the headlines are 'British indie-rock guy goes ape-shit in New York hotel' kind of thing. But two hours later George Michael got arrested. So that was the main news. I was a footnote at that point. Thank God.

They charged me with third-degree assault and harassment relating to Julia. Once there they put me in the tombs with all these black fellows, this *Sopranos*-type guy and this six foot two kid from San Francisco; his racket involved picking up rich gay New York guys, going back to their houses, hitting them over the head and nicking their credit cards. He rang his mam up as well to bring him back home.

The cell's the size of a small living room and there's about twenty fellows in there, and they kept turning the lights on and off all the time. You can't get any sleep, you're all stood up. Then they transfer you to another cell. The Italian guy's shouting out, 'Police cruelty! Police cruelty!' all the time.

Then we had to go down and watch a film together just before we went to Rikers Island. We were sat behind school desks, and they started showing us these three films. There's obviously a police analyst behind a screen, gauging our reaction. There's about forty of us and this copper asks us what films we would like to watch. First one's this *Little House on the Prairie* type of film, and everybody starts groaning. 'Or you can watch this one, guys,' says this copper. And it's your regular police drama like *Hill Street Blues* or something. Everybody starts booing when the guy catches the criminal. And then it's, 'What about this one?' Two fellows beating the shit out of each other, and everybody goes, 'Weahh!' It's this really bad fake boxing match. Some of the black guys, hardened crims, are like, 'What kind of prison is this – you've only got three channels?' And it's clearly not on telly like these coppers are making out, but some of the cons in there thought it was, because they're not the type to be watching TV – too busy selling coke. It's this fake boxing match! It seems funny now, but not then; then, my bowels were liquid with fear. This went on for about an hour and a half, but it was at least a relief that we didn't have to sit in the cell.

Then they read out all the names, and all of them are wrong; and of course Smith turns up in every arrest form. They got everything wrong – that's why my bail was fucked up. They had the boat waiting for Rikers, and they're coming in reading out the wrong batch of prisoners. They're reading out these names and nobody's replying and then they read out Smith and I'm the only one who said yeah. And they're all laughing at this, because there's always a Smith somewhere, but this wasn't me, it was Sylvester Smith or something, Sly Stone Smith. They couldn't even get this right, which was quite frightening.

And then they brought these urine samples out, these tubes with everybody's name on them.

'Wilson – what's in your urine?' And he goes, 'I don't know, and I don't care.' And then onto the Puerto Ricans, and theirs is all pure. And then they get to this black guy and he's got it all – VD, the clap, crack, heroin, this green scum, the lot – all in this tube. And some of the guys are saying, 'That's our Bo-Bo, always flying the flag!' and the guy in question's slumped down, dribbling, saying, 'Well, it was a good night.' Then it's the black gang guys and theirs is all very pure, with about 1 per cent coke in there. Come to mine and there's about 90 per cent alcohol in there, pure white alcohol. Obviously. I'd not had anything to eat in two days. The place erupts after this. 'Look at the limey's piss!' they're shouting, clapping hands.

They're so incompetent, the Yanks, I was only meant to be in there for a night, not two, and they were just about to shave my head for Rikers Island. I was stripped off and everything. Luckily, five minutes before I was due to go, my bail came through.

And so as I'm going out all the coppers are holding their hands out, saying good luck, acting all nice – like I'm James Bond. It reminded me of when they liberated the British concentration camps, when the SS put their hands out and the British just blanked them.

So I walk out and it's 5 o'clock in the morning, no money, no cigs, and I have to come back at 11 o'clock for my passport. Just walking around, wandering, picking up cig dimps.

I'm outside the World Trade Center, and it's about 9 a.m. now, so I've got another hour or so to waste. I've got a tweed jacket on, I'm not looking scruffy; looked really well, in fact, not having had a drink for a few days.

And this copper comes over and says, 'Can you move on?' like *Top Cat*, and I say, 'No, I can't move on, I need shelter from the rain, I've just come from the tombs, I need my passport, and my money.'

So he let me stay there for a bit. To keep him talking I said, 'Can you tell me about these two buildings here, my father's a builder and there's one side here that hasn't got a joist on it, how many people are in there?'

And he says, 'Well, they should know what they're doing – there's 3,000 of them in there.'

I said, 'They better watch it, they haven't got a lintel or a joist.' This is what holds the side of your house up, it's the main support. I could tell this because all the other buildings would sway slightly in the ordinary wind, but not this one.

And this copper just goes, 'Never really thought about it,' and walks off.

At this stage I need a light, so I'm going, 'Excuse me, sir, have you got a light on you?' and this guy goes, 'Smoking's for losers.'

Once the rain had stopped I had to get to SoHo. I asked this other guy where it was and he says, 'No, I don't know where it is, you fucking hippy.'

But just like the arrogant fucker before, he was going into the World Trade Center as well.

Aftermath

The bottom end of it was that the New York court said I had to go on this alcohol programme, twice a week for six weeks in Bury.

But the staff there seemed to have more problems than I had. I didn't have any problems, to be quite honest. I don't think I did.

I had to fill in this form about how much I drank – units per week etc. The lawyer in America would be ringing me asking me about the reports. So I write down the truth. British doctors think if you say you smoke ten cigs a week, it's more like fifty. But I told the truth because it was for New York, not the Bury NHS.

America is really down on drink. I always believe in being open with things like that. These people who are lecturing you, journalists and whatnot, they're all out of their heads on Charlie. I can tell by their pupils. I'll say to them, do you fancy a drink? And they say, I'll come with you but I'll just have a coffee. And then you get a beer down them and they'll start telling you everything. How they have a joint before they go to work, how they're on uppers, downers, Charlie, the lot; but because you've got four cans in your hand, it's not acceptable. You can see it from their point of view: you can't go into an office in New York with a can and a bottle of whisky.

But the guys who worked in this alcohol programme place couldn't understand that drinking four or five cans of Holsten Pils a day – which is what I was doing – is not like drinking four or five cans of Special Brew. They'd be like, 'Isn't it?' I soon realized that most of them who worked there were all ex-E-heads. They'd say to me, 'Here's some literature that might help you,' and it's all these Furry Freak Brothers-style comics about 'Gary the E-head from Bolton', on how you shouldn't take E every day.

I remember reading them: 'Gary goes out on a Saturday and Sunday and takes a few Es then he sits at home all week,' and you've got all these thought bubbles coming out of his head, all these worries like 'Poll Tax and Rent!' And I'm going, 'What good's this to me?' Basically it was a pamphlet on how to take E responsibly: eat fruit and veg all week, get your sleep, party at the weekend . . .

And this is not what the New York court wanted to see.

It's funny, though, I quite enjoyed it there. You'd have these Scottish guys stood outside with these young Bury lads, and the Scottish guys would be saying, 'Get in there, laddy! Instead of stealing cider from Tesco's, just get four Special Brew and some drugs from in there – say you're addicted to the cider; and you combine the drugs with the Special Brew. Young laddy like you will only need a couple of cans a day and not be raiding your mammy's purse.'

And the lads would be like, 'Er . . . alright, I'll think about that, yeah.' We're talking about kids who'd been drinking washing-up liquid, anything.

But they didn't even know about the anger-management

programme. They just asked me questions like, 'Why are you angry?', or said things like, 'Oh, you must be surrounded by drugs when you're in a studio.' And I said, 'No, I have a ban on drugs in the studio.' And they'd say, 'Is that why you're angry then?'

I had to explain to them that I get angry because I'd go into the studio and the engineer can't sort out the fucking guitar overdubs because he's had eight joints, or he's on heroin or coke – the latter is a special problem as it affects the ears. Or you'll do a good track and say, come on lads put the Rizlas away, we'll go and have a pint. And they say, 'Oh no, it's alright, we'll stay here and watch telly, you go to the pub, Mark.' Engineers and producers are the same. All the time I get this.

So I'll go out, come back; I've not been to the pub, and I can hear them saying, 'He'll be back in a minute, shouting from the pub.' And I'll come in, pretend I'm pissed and go, 'Have you done that track yet?' And they'll go, 'You don't understand, it's the computer.' When it's not the computer; when in fact they've just had a few lines, thinking I don't know. It's a particularly middle-class thing, like secret drinkers.

I'm always the scapegoat.

Afterwards, I got this letter off my lawyer, saying, 'Dear New York court, Mr Smith was on a six-week course, we had twelve appointments and he only turned up for six of them, Yours, Yvonne.'

I had to ring them up and say, what the fuck are you doing? For a start off I went to nine or ten of the appointments. So I had to write the letter for her. Unbelievable. She's so used to writing out letters for the British courts, she didn't seem to realize the seriousness of the situation. I had to do all the work for them, send it off, and thankfully it was alright.

It's sort of good for me, though, this idea that I'm a mad drunk. It makes people frightened of me.

People are always trying to diagnose it . . .

A lot of women journalists in particular see it as a self-destructive tendency.

Everything's going well and I press the button 'DESTROY'. It's all going too well. Today I'm going to self-destruct. Like the serial-shagger who floats from house to house setting up families and then buggering off into the night; and so on. And fellows see a bit too much of themselves in me and would rather ignore it or go the other way and tell all and sundry what a nightmare I am, behind my back. I don't know how football managers go on with all that malarkey – or how my dad and my grandad coped with it.

But when it's artistic – it's a bit harder still. You've got to find a level with them. It's a constant battle.

There's been many a time when a band member has panicked before going on tour – they've left their passport at home or they're just too frightened of the unknown. What annoys me is that they don't think I have the same fears. They're so self-centred, these fellows, they don't think I shit myself when we're on tour and it's all icy and I'm responsible for six people in a van and the driver's pissed out of his head.

I've been on planes with group members and they're literally shitting themselves. They think I'm mad because I'm still talking away or chewing tobacco. Two days before I was due to fly out on the 2006 American tour I had one of those really realistic dreams about a plane crash, the residue of which was still lingering in my head when I was in the airport . . . But you just get on. You have to. They don't seem to have any pride like that. That's not manly to me. You see them next time and it's as if nothing's happened.

I really do think they see me as a robot, or as insane, or suicidal. I get it in pubs. I'm a living caricature. I've been out with gangsters, coked out of their heads, taking the piss, and I've just put them in their place. And fellows are saying, 'Do

you know who that is? You're mad, you.' I don't feel like I've
done anything out of the ordinary. It's a blessing in one respect.
I can walk down the street and nobody will bother me. It's held
me in good stead. I can walk down a trendy London street and
they know who I am, but they don't come up to me.

I can empty a bar – a really heavy vault. If I apply my mind I
can clear it. If I'm doing an interview and it gets busy I can clear
that room.

I don't know what it is. I don't give out heavy vibes. There
must be a feeling around me: the simmer . . .

18. Crisp Man

I'm a bit like the Alex Ferguson of the music game. I see parallels with his timing. He knows when to fuck players off – none of that pandering to reputations. It's his club. His ideas. His final word. And the results are evident.

If only City could get him. He's the one they need; never going to happen, but he'd definitely sort them out. When he got rid of David Beckham everybody thought he was mad – 'Beckham's in his prime' and all that shit. But Ferguson stayed strong and got on with his job, improving his team. There's a lot to be said for that, for not listening too much to people outside of the loop. I get it a lot, but I never pay any attention; record company people thinking I haven't a clue what I'm doing – that I'm too drunk to sort the important things out; totally overlooking the fact I've been doing it a lot longer than they have. It's not a bad thing in some ways. The amount of times I've pulled an album out of the shitter when they've not expected it – like the *Infotainment Scan* and *The Real New Fall* and *Reformation*.

They wanted Ferguson's head at one stage as well. Typical Man United.

Having said that, I could have told City that Stuart Pearce was the wrong man ages ago. I saw him on a plane once; he looked deranged then. All that running up and down the pitch and firing up the fans – that's had its day, that shit. He's been mingling with the Keegans too much: the dated English. City are at their best when they're in-between managers; when they've got something to prove; uncertainty seems to bring the best out of them. Nobody wants an England reject at the helm, though. They're damaged personalities. Some managers see that as the pinnacle of their careers; imagine how they feel when it's all gone tits-up? They're hardly going to be brimming with enthusiasm and new ideas.

I couldn't believe it when they hired that hod-carrier Steve McLaren – he reminds me of one of those blokes who starts to panic if he's not occupying his mind with a catalogue of small things; the sort you see out in the garden every sunny Sunday – oblivious to what really matters.

I did like it in the 2006 World Cup though when he was wearing those really tight shorts; I liked the way they seemed to be glued to his legs. Imagine hiring a fellow who dresses like that! That's the English FA for you. Let's get somebody cheap in after we've blown all our dough on Sven. And then they went and hired Terry Venables too. To me that's hilarious. What was it the judge said about him being unfit to be a director of a company? How can they let people like that back in?

I never support England. Me and Elena loved it when Greece won the Euro 2004 final. England will never be able to play like that, as a team, all working for each other. Not when your club managers are ten times savvier.

You can bet some strange things go on behind the doors of the FA. They're like a cult; a randy cult souped up on good wine, expensive fruit and nice clean sausages. Just look back throughout the history – overlooking Brian Clough in favour of Ron Greenwood, for instance. You can't legislate for minds like that. It's as if defeat is ingrained in them – as if they can only handle defeat. It's the English malaise to plump for second best; they get frightened by the prospect of sustained success – that and the fact they don't know what they're talking about when it comes to football. They didn't want Clough in there because he had a gob on him and he liked a drink and he openly refused to take any shit. And the more they tried to gag him the more he blurted. Men like that are not going to be strait-jacketed; they are who they are. Simple.

I just find it funny how men in England talk about football. I remember being in a pub, and Ben walked in with a few of his mates; he used to play in some five-a-side league or other. But you should have heard the way they were speaking – everything they said was infected by TV pundits, every word. They were talking like they'd just been playing for Real Madrid, analysing passes – 'And did you see it when I beat that defender,' and 'If only he would have crossed it quicker.' On and on, and really loud, about some fucking game they'd just played in Bury. I was with a mate of mine. I felt embarrassed.

When I wrote 'Kicker Conspiracy' in '83 nobody gave a fuck about football. I got called a hooligan for writing that song. *Melody Maker* said I must have writer's block for knocking rubbish like that out. Football was exclusively working class then. It was a serious stain on the English landscape at one point.

I have a feeling that that side of it – the football hoolie side – is on its way back now that English teams have started doing well in Europe. That's how it all started in the first place.

But then in the early 90s football got annexed by a bunch of Walter Softies. The middle class just lifted it – stole it wholesale. After the '90 World Cup, when that fat child Gazza balled his eyes out, it became a soap opera – like *Coronation Street*. Now it's a tool for the middle classes. I'm not saying the working class have completely deserted it, but it's very much a middle-class hobby now. Drips like Nick Hornby and David Baddiel and Damon Albarn have a lot to answer for. As soon as they started in on it with their university humour, it shot its bolt. Don't get me wrong, I still watch it. But twenty years ago you would never have dreamed of today's annexation.

There was never any need to go down this path. I noticed the early signs when I wrote 'Kicker', but I never imagined it'd become so cynical and anti-communal. They hike the price of tickets in order to have it for themselves. And that's not football;

that's not thousands of people sharing in something. Not if you can't afford it.

There must be millions of people who've had to completely alter their lives because of it. I used to go myself in the 80s, when it was all standing, as it should be now. You don't sit down to watch a game of football. You sit down to watch a film or ballet or swimming, not a bunch of blokes belting a ball and each other around. I can't hold with that.

Even ticket prices at clubs like Bury, who are unmistakably crap, are top-heavy. I used to watch them for free in the 80s. I'd walk through this knackered cemetery and jump the fence – they weren't worth paying for then, it's eighteen quid now!

It should be looked into a lot more than it actually is. Take Leeds – nobody's really dug the dirt on that moneyed debacle. Somebody must know where it all went. They were like the Factory Records of football, with this wealth of talent on their doorstep and a stack of bills the size of their own deception.

How can anybody truly follow somebody who's on £100,000 a week? I don't begrudge them the money; if they're good they're good and I'd rather a working-class lad had it than some slippery Ken, like it used to be. The simple fact is, though, money's clouded the heart of the matter. When you're earning cash like that you're not going to be out there playing for your life. All you have to do is compare any of the recent teams with Alf Ramsey's England. They were real men. They even looked like real men.

I think it's a shame that kids are growing up with that sort of accepted corruption in football. Football for me was always a bit of escapism. You didn't watch it to be reminded of your spiralling tax debt; you watched it because it was about blokes giving their all on an afternoon, regardless of dough. Funny how the problem coincided with the anti-drink brigade – as soon as they eradicated that side of it, it became a money show. They sucked the camaraderie out of it at the same time. Now when they have a drink it's in some gaudy bar in Soho and they've got five security guys tagging along. George Best never did that, and he was the first of the real celebrity footballers. He drank alone or with his mates.

I always buy *When Saturday Comes*, the football magazine. It's very good. They ran this brilliant piece on football autobiographies just after the 2006 World Cup; how most of them got sent back and how Cashley Cole sold fourteen copies of his. But the interesting thing about it was the way in which these publishers put their faith in these berks. I mean, they were never going to win that World Cup; and never underestimate people's reaction after something like that. You can't shit on your country like they did, crying and fluffing penalties, and then expect some call-centre jockey to go out and devour your book for eighteen quid. But that's the esteem these people are held in.

The Dudes got a fright when all that kicked off. It was the first weekend of the World Cup and they'd just flown in from LA to Manchester; we were playing the New Century Hall that night. Jet-lagged and frazzled, their first English sight is a bunch of pissed-up England fans with seared faces falling over and mauling each other.

Hilarious. It was one of the hottest days of the year. Everywhere they went they were confronted by pissed-up men, half-starkers, yelling football songs.

'Is this normal?'

I was pissing myself. Fat blokes on heat screaming 'Rooney!'

It's amazing the power these players have over some fellows: the hold. It's very homoerotic. We're talking about blokes with mortgages and shrieking kids. I don't think they're that bothered about their wives. They seem to get off on football more; football and Carling and themselves.

It's the same with the likes of Elton John and those guys off *Little Britain*. They're beyond royalty in a way. Elton John has more clout than the Prime Minister. All he's ever done is bung a few quid Watford's way. (I was inspired by him, actually. I was thinking of buying Bury football club when they were in the shit a couple of years ago. It would have only cost me about £2,000.) It's astonishing how he's become a whole new medium in himself, because he never really says anything. He's become the king of the New Homosexual Elite all of a sudden. It's tricky ground, but he seems to be the head of all that stuff about inspecting people's wardrobes and kitchens, telling them how out of date and clueless they are for still having brass in their living room. And somehow people have bought into it and he's beyond TV and even fucking music. He can literally do what he pleases.

I've done interviews where I've been purposefully arsey. It can be quite amusing. But I've only resorted to it when the interviewer's not prepared properly. It's usually a bloke. I don't like doing interviews with women; they always fall on their arse. It never feels right. They never know what to say to me.

But it's not always that clear-cut. A lot of the time these things get distorted. When I did that interview with Michael Bracewell at the ICA in London in '94, the critics wrote it up as a complete balls-up along the lines of me being pissed and uncaring; and Bracewell being out of his league. The hacks lay in wait on that one. I wasn't pissed. The first half of it went okay. Maybe some of the questions were overly academic, but that's what he is; he wanted to get down with this idea of the 'self-taught artist'. That was the crux of it.

I've nothing against him. I think he's good. But he's another casualty, he worries that he's over-pretentious. Compared to Paul Morley and most other writers Bracewell's an artist.

There was a hell of a lot of media people in that night, and not many fans. And most of them had had a fair few. As soon as I sat down I got the feeling they weren't taking it seriously.

Like always, they were just there to see me make an idiot of myself. As soon as Bracewell had finished his questions he asked the audience if they had any questions and the first person to speak was a half-cut hack:

'Yes, I'd like to know if you're still a piss-head, Mark.'

That shows the calibre of journalists I was contending with that night. I had a few bottles of beer with me in a bag and a few on the table, I suppose that's why he asked it.

But it's hardly a good starting point, is it?

After that I couldn't be arsed. It was a pointless exercise. But it's not a big issue. I'm surprised it still gets written about. It was just another failed interview. I'm sure I'll be at the centre of a few more.

Bracewell shouldn't be bothered about it, to be honest. He tried his best on a bad night. That's all you can say about it. As for his writing, he's one of the better cultural commentators. He doesn't jump in with the pack as much as the other so-called journalists.

It says a lot about them when they start harping on about the lack of real heroes nowadays; and how fame has been cheapened by the likes of The Spice Girls and reality-TV contestants. What they don't realize is that most of the people they revere – people like Elton John and Mick Jagger and John Lennon – are or were cunts.

Mel C seems an alright person to me. At least she never acted like an imperialist in America, unlike Lennon. He was already very arrogant, but when he met Yoko and started doing all that public protest malarkey it became an amplified arrogance. You can't go to a foreign country and act like that; thumbing your nose to the government. In their eyes he was just a hop-head with these silly ideas about equality and peace. He'd stopped living in the real world; at least when he was in The Beatles he had something to concentrate on. In the end he just became a bag of loose ideas. There was an element of madness in him;

voicing principles like that but living the life he did. He got away with it because of his music.

They were a horrible, conceited bunch, that 70s lot – Elton John, Clapton and Bowie. It's indicative of the age we're living in that they're still revered the way they are, when our recent Prime Minister wishes he was one of them.

I have a great problem with elevating people like this. I still try to steer the group away from that world. I used to be more forceful in this respect. Last thing anybody wants to be doing is bumming up a bunch of rich musicians. This should be obvious. The only people I ever really looked up to were Link Wray and Iggy Pop, but that was then and I was in the minority there . . .

And Harry Dowd of course. He was as far removed from the modern footballer as you're going to get. He was City's goalkeeper in the Championship-winning team in 1968. He was brilliant. Funny bastard as well. He worked as a plumber, like my dad. He'd come and talk to us at games; plumbing talk, copper joints and drain unblockers and all that . . . He knew what he was talking about, too. His mind was a lot sharper than Frank Lampard's.

What I do love about football is the shirt brigade. The pundits: Alan Hansen and Alan Shearer and crisp man Gary Lineker. I like the way they all wear their open-necked, big-collared shirts in a casual style. I bet they all shop together. Ring each other up before they're due on, asking which colour they're going to be wearing tonight. It's that uniform mentality again. Policemen are the same. You can spot a cop party miles away. Michael Owen and Alan Shearer look like policemen as well.

It was funny when *Grandstand* asked me to read the final scores out. I think it all came about from this girl who was working for Peel as an administrator before he died. She was transferred from there. Apparently, Ray Stubbs is a big fan. He was alright. He's very good when he's presenting the darts. Whereas other fellows would just take the piss and do it in a tongue-in-cheek way, he throws himself into it. It's a different world, the sports world – there comes a time when you're speaking to those sports people and you start thinking they're on a different planet altogether.

The producer woman was really smart and sharp, taking me round, telling me what everybody does, pointing out Mark Lawrenson and Crisp Man.

'And this is Carlton Palmer. And this is Garth Crooks, and this is what they do and I'll see you later.'

They were all strapped down to their chairs at this stage with their shirts on.

After she'd buggered off they assigned me these two women. But they had to do it in shifts. I was supposed to watch the second half of the City match, but of course I couldn't do that. I kept walking off to the bar. Even if I was at the game I wouldn't watch the second half. We're not talking a United fan here, analysing every second of the game.

And this first girl is pointing out every nook and cranny. Because they have a load of daft soccer players walking around the place who haven't a clue where they're going, people like Bryan Robson. But I'm trying to tell her that I know where I'm going, that I've been here a few times. Then she starts getting visibly annoyed.

It's a Saturday afternoon, remember. She obviously wanted to be somewhere else. Shopping. Not watching me drink a pint.

And then this other girl turns up, a Jo Whiley-ite, who only wanted to talk about Oasis.

'Have you ever met the Gallaghers then?'

I'm on my third pint at this stage. 'No, love.'

Talking about festivals and Noel, and that the last festival she went to she happened to see Liam. I just wanted a bit of peace.

'Wouldn't you rather be somewhere else? I won't tell anybody if you just leave me here and do a bit of shopping . . .'

Saturday's a very holy day for me – I don't like working on

a Saturday still. I never have. It's my day off. Start at twelve and drink all day. I've always done that since I was sixteen. Play records. Piss around. Go out for a pint.

'Oh, I can't do that. I've got to make sure you get back.'

And she kept reminding me how long I had left before I was due to read the scores out.

'Only twenty minutes to go now . . .'

And then this big Jamaican woman barges in. 'Mr Smith, you now have to go to room something or other. They'll be waiting for you.'

There were more people working behind the scenes than on the pitch!

And of course the game itself was a load of fucking cack; worst City game since the last.

Garth Crooks was a good bloke, though. He was asking me about Kevin Keegan. I told him that I thought he was shit; that if you were to split him open he'd have 'loser' imprinted down the middle, like lettering in Blackpool rock.

I find it quite funny that they're using 'Sparta' on the programme. It's hardly a friendly football song. But I'm glad that it's on there. I always used to watch *Final Score*. I don't see it as selling out – as long as you get paid enough. I think people have a completely different notion of selling out from me. Selling out to me is compromising the sound of your music, or watering down your lyrics so they read stale.

It was a bit different when they used 'Touch Sensitive' for that Vauxhall Corsa advert. I didn't have full control over that. And at the time I needed the money. Sometimes that's the sad case. We're not all Elton John.

The good thing about 'Sparta' is that it's reached a new audience. I hear a lot of people have got into The Fall from tuning in to see how Raith Rovers went on against Kilmarnock. Football's the new religion in that sense: the opium of the masses. You could really subvert it – beam subliminal messages through Chelsea. I reckon they'd be up for it as well. They're already halfway there. They've already dragged other clubs into the money race. They can do anything they want. Watch out!

All done now, anyway. Another mobile to investigate. More names for The List. More gone. He said G.B. may even drop the uniform off personally. And then a line enters my head like an axe, 'Beware of all enterprises that require new clothes' . . .

19. To Hell and Back

The Marshall Suite (1999) was my glorious return after the New York ordeal. John Lennard, who'd managed us on and off since '85 and who was an all-round decent bloke, was the only guy who'd touch me at that stage. He was pretty good. He took a bit of advantage, but I wasn't in a position of any power. Nobody gave a fuck about me – 'Big mouth Smith falls on his arse again!' I wasn't bothered about that at all. They had a point.

John just said, 'We can't have you not recording' – which was nice. We'd left him in nasty circumstances after the *Middle Class Revolt* LP in '94. I think he was under the impression that we were U2 and that we'd go on to sell enough records to go out together and buy a house each.

But he was now on his uppers a bit and he just wanted me to do an LP.

I asked for the best studio in London and he paid for it. But he didn't tell me that I wasn't going to get any money. That's London for you; he's a Chelsea boy, John. I got about £100 every three days but not a cent off the album.

But there's not many labels who'd have helped me out like that. I'll always be grateful to Artful for getting in touch. It's not like I asked them to do it. It couldn't have been an easy decision for them. The whole group were a bit bonkers at the time. I wasn't any better, but Neville Wilding and Julia – we're not talking stable personalities here.

It wasn't a stable period in England full stop. I remember doing an interview with *Loaded* magazine in '97. One of my best interviews, in fact. It's still talked about now. I was pretty pissed and this *Loaded* fellow was very persistent and very boring, and so I sabotaged the whole thing. But it was exactly what they wanted. All those journalists used to try to provoke chaos in me – well, that was it in motion. I knew what I was doing. I thought he was shit. That's why I called him a cretin and a frustrated pervert. That's all *Loaded* ever was – a semi-porn mag, like the porn mags in the 70s. Everybody was reading it in secret – *NME* writers, *Guardian* writers . . .

As soon as you question these people, it's a big deal. Beforehand, you're the rebel, the cool rebel, then once you do or say something that doesn't include them they distance themselves. It's alright having a go at obvious things, at fucking Wet Wet Wet or Take That, but once you question the worth of their own so-called rebel mag they don't like it.

Funniest part of it was at the end, when Ash tried to start on me. Pathetic; this bunch of de-balled soft-arse college rockers getting all uppity. Not an idea between them, poor lads.

At the time, I thought it was the end of my career. Everybody who'd read it said I'd blown it. It's funny to me.

But 1997 was like the death of innocence. You only have to look at it now; England will never back a politician in the way they did Tony Blair; they were the last days of all that shit. And Diana; what was all that about? She was the perfect martyr for the times, in that she never stood for anything, never did anything. The same people who talk about shitty celebrities now could be seen signing her condolence book back then in 1997. It sounds harsh, but death saved her in a way. I'm not against the royals actually. They are what they are; and most of the time they're not the real problem. It wasn't long after that that *Friends* became the new religion. After believing in Blair and after being sold down the river by him, people turned to this daft American comedy. You can see where the 'shoulder to shoulder' thing came in with Blair and Bush; it was little more than an extension of Blair watching too much of that shit. I'd go into pubs and there'd be groups of women and men acting like these characters. Single men were suddenly seen as a genuine threat. Cultural brainwash . . . The idea of *Friends*, of this bunch of well-to-do New Yorkers, was an idyllic head-trip for people, in the same way that pot entered middle-class suburban America in the 70s after Watergate. After which these people turned into the 'SS Frappuccino'; purveyors of froth and enemies of Nescafé.

England hasn't recovered from that year. I have; but England hasn't. They bought into something so faithfully with the Labour Party that they're still reeling from the after-effects. Sunshine and well-spoken promises does this to people. The day that Blair won out, when all the cameras were privy to the new dawn and the sun was shining, that'll be filed alongside Nazi propaganda in the future.

It's always the same when you've got a writer or a musician who's hit a low but isn't willing to start creeping to their so-called betters. That's what they wanted me to do after '98. They wanted me to fall in line and become a 'friend' of theirs, to hang around with them in the hospitality tents, drinking and snorting lines; one more paid-up member of their all-boys club . . . Fuck that. I knew what I had to do and I did it. *The Marshall Suite*'s still a good album. I'll stand by that one. It must have annoyed certain people when it was released, because the general consensus was I'd had it; no more comebacks for Mad Mark, and all that.

That's how they treated Malcolm Lowry, the writer. Left to rot because he didn't think like them.

When you're in a loop, your behaviour is constantly being assessed. You might not realize it, but there'll come a time when you're hit in the face with it. After all the shit I'd been through with Julia, New York and that poxy *Loaded* interview, it happened to me at Glastonbury. It seemed like a small thing, but it happens like that. It's not necessarily the big things in life, like love and death, but the small moments.

We'd just finished playing and Bob Dylan was on after us. I'd been standing on stage playing to all these idiot fans. And it's going nowhere. So we wrapped it up. It's a nice day and the group had fucked off to see Bob – being musos. And I fell fast asleep as soon as he started playing. It was about 8 o'clock. Bob's droning on and I'm konked out near the pre-fabs and the dressing-room huts. There was nobody around. It was the only peace I'd had all day. I've got my hands behind my head, thinking, 'Ah – no mitherers . . .' And just as I'm drifting off I hear . . .

'Mark! Mark! Mark!'

. . . this big, stupid voice. And there's Vic Reeves and Bob Mortimer and a journalist who I can't remember.

'Come on, Mark. You can't do this.'

'What? What can't I do?' I wanted a lie-down.

'What you doing, Mark – do you know what you're doing?'

'Yeah . . . I'm having a kip.'

'Come on, Mark, don't lose it. Come to the celebrity tent and watch him with us. Don't do this to yourself.'

Journalists and cameramen are walking past now, after hearing Vic Reeves' big mouth.

Bob Mortimer's going, 'Come on, Marky! You don't have to go in the crowd.'

I think I had a lot of white powder up my nose. They were looking out for me in a way, because I wasn't hanging out at the hospitality tent. And they walked off, no doubt thinking, 'Oh, it's a shame for him. No going back now . . .' As if I was some old blues singer whose best days were over – 'He had it all at one point, now look at him: falling asleep next to an empty Portakabin.' We never played any festivals after that. Vic Reeves never rang me again. Don't know why not. He used to ring me a lot, even wanted to record something with me at one stage. But that was the end of that.

Things like that don't bother me. I'm not in it to be like

them. I know who my mates are, and that's more than a lot of others do.

I always used to have an entourage when I played Manchester. Because it can go either way – people can be looking out for you, like Vic and Bob, or they can have a few drinks and start acting like Chuck Norris.

Some Salford lads always used to come to gigs with me. They're all good lads, they'd do anything for me, and they don't even like The Fall. What I'm saying is that you do need protection when you're playing those council gigs in Manchester, with their rules about bouncers, about people having to have licences to be this, that and the other, because there's always some mad bird from Chorlton on E who you shagged twenty years ago who's trying to come up to you with a knife. And the bouncers are either reconstructed criminals who are only bothered about what you've got in your wallet, or they're gym teachers. You go backstage and there's about twenty-five of them sat in front of their computers not giving a fuck. Anything can happen up there.

I've always had loyal people around The Fall. You don't want too many fans on the inside, because they'd rather be watching the show than keeping their eyes peeled for head-cases.

Those lads really helped me out. And not just at gigs, but with LPs as well; like *Are You are Missing Winner* (2001) – they were there throughout the recording. Ben can talk all he likes about the atmosphere of the times; how shit the studio was and how I never turned up, etc., etc.

We got the studio on the cheap, I'll admit that. But it was good – the spirit was there. It's not as if he moaned about it at the time. We could only get in for four hours at a time. We all chipped in, all the Salford mob; even Sean Bainey, our manager then – even he was good; same goes for Jim Watts and Spencer. It wasn't a nightmare. And then Ben goes on to say how the album wasn't very good. Then why didn't he say something? I played him the LP and his reaction was typical: 'I'm not saying anything, you're the boss.'

That wasn't an easy time for me or for the group, and we all stuck in there. But the way he talks about it now it's as if he's wasted five years of his life on The Fall. And it wasn't always shit.

Just before *Are you are Missing Winner* was released, we'd booked this tour of America. We were broke and we wanted to get back there. We got offered this tour – two gigs in LA and two or three in New York. We'd already booked the tickets, but in between 9/11 happened. But we needed the money at the time. There was no way we were not going to go. It turned out to be the only time we played America and came back with any money. When we got to LA we played two nights at this place but every other British and American group had cancelled all their shows. Everybody came trundling in once they found out that we were the only band in town and that all the others had cancelled. We were on a fucking roll.

But in New York, Sean had found us this bloody stupid hotel overlooking the 9/11 site. This Armenian place. It was dead cheap. You couldn't open the windows, the stench was that bad.

We got a day off on the weekend. And we're all glad to be there; surprised, in fact, they'd even let us in the country, because we'd cancelled a lot of American tours and a lot of people had cancelled on us since that jail business. So we didn't go just for the money this time. If we hadn't played then that would have been the nail in the coffin for the States. Because there was another idiot – a total phoney who put up tour dates for America on the sites a few months beforehand and we never had any intention of going there. So this time it would have been the fourth time we'd jipped out.

Thank fuck we didn't . . .

We had money in our pockets for the first time in ages and

so we all went out for a drink in New York. I'll never forget it. We'd been in America for a week but not really noticed it – because we'd been busy. The smell was unimaginably grim. It's weird with The Fall – everywhere we bloody go there's always something. I just said, 'Let's get out of this area. Let's go to Wall Street.'

We went on the main drag and I swear seven out of every ten men had a uniform on: coppers, marines, national guards, park rangers, boy scouts, paratroopers . . . we really stood out as the only civilians. Everybody was looking at us, especially at Sean, because he was unshaven.

We were a bit feisty, though.

'What are they looking at us for?'

All the old timers have come in for the Sunday afternoon – dug their old uniforms out of the cupboard.

None of the rubbish had been cleaned up. And there were all these ghouls around the rubble. Not one of them is helping. No fucker's doing anything.

The fire station they had around there was like *Camberwick Green* – it's farcical considering the money they've got.

Gradually, Sean's accent changes and he starts talking about his Irish roots and all this shit. He suddenly changes into *Gangs of New York*. As soon as he gets to Wall Street, he's turning round shouting, 'I told you this tour would turn out well, Mark.' We had thousands of dollars in our pockets. Not before or since have we ever had so much money. He was like Jimmy Cagney.

'It's fantastic! Top of the world, Ma!'

'What's fantastic, Sean? Everybody's got a uniform on.'

And he says 'Let's have an old drink, to celebrate.' So we go into this Irish bar on Wall Street. Not a proper Irish bar, of course. William Fitzpatrick and Patrick Fitzwilliams, as we used to say. We walk in the bar through these double doors and he starts walking like Popeye. Inside, there's all these rich Irish guys in suits. Barman pulls this morose expression; not being in a good mood at that particular time of the year. After that thing, I don't think they were in the right mood for anybody. Least of all the new American Sean . . .

'Hello there, my son,' he says in this ridiculous New York-Irish accent. I'm thinking – what's he playing at?

He walks over to this strapping guy in a suit. 'I'll have a pint of Guinness and three pints of lager for my English friends.'

I thought, you fucking twat! And the barman says, 'I'm not serving you. Under New York law I don't serve people like you who have obviously lost their senses. I'll give you the lagers, though – for your buddies.'

I was pissing myself.

There were all these concert posters of Morrissey on the streets as well. Just his big face looking out at you from every other corner. And Sean was just high out of his head – he'd never been to New York before.

'Yeah, it's really weird – that jet-lag: I keep thinking I'm seeing pictures of my Uncle George everywhere I go.'

Apparently his Uncle George looks like Morrissey.

I was saying, it's a surreal environment to walk into after coming from LA, what with all these uniforms and rubble and the overriding smell.

And Sean's like, 'I know how you feel, Mark. I've not seen Uncle George in ages.'

It was a great tour, though. The lads had played well and we all came back with a few quid. After that it hit me that it might be a good idea to start re-building The Fall again. Not that I was ever going to quit. I'd just come to the end of a lot of shit, and there was something there with the lads that I felt was worth pursuing. And it was like that for a time. Something like *Country on the Click: The Real New Fall LP* (2003), that came from nowhere. I know for a fact that people were surprised by its quality. We'd been written off again and nobody expected us to come back with something as good as that.

I went through a lot of shit trying to get it out. We nearly signed to Mute at one stage. What a palaver that was! They were always interfering and fucking about with it. We had to do it all again in Manchester. And it was the same thing there – cunts coming down from London, knocking on my door on spec because they just happened to be in the area; asking me when the LP's ready.

In the end I just told them to fuck off. They never did any work. Sat there asking me what 'Sparta' is about. I spent three months with them – used up half their money, and half my money. It was a farce. I'm too proud to beg – that's the problem. I'd rather fund myself than go asking for three days' studio money.

That's why we had to go to Action records.

As is always the case, the problems began when Ben and Steve started grumbling about credits. In their minds they did everything. They can't just be in a group – they want it all. And as soon as *Fall Heads Roll* (2005) was released and the reviews came in, they wanted all the credit for it. The thing that bothers me is when they actually believe it themselves. It's alright telling every ear in the vicinity that you've done this, this and this – if they want to believe you, then fair enough. But when it gets to a stage where you start believing it yourself, then you're just deluded. But for me, *Fall Heads Roll* would have been a mess. I was the one who brought it together. There's a thread in that LP I was trying to get at. The group didn't even realize this. I always wanted to make an album that had a thread of words and that's what *Fall Heads Roll* is – I think so, anyway.

It gets quite maudlin in a way, quite depressing. I thought about trying to tart it up a bit, but it seemed best just to leave it. About three quarters of the way through making it some people were saying it's getting quite hard, this; and I'm just telling them to stick with it. That's what I wanted to do.

Sound-wise it was difficult as well. You had every Tom, Dick and Harry interfering: 'What about this and that and that and do this one and put this there.' It's worse than it's ever been for things like that. You get A&R men thinking they can sort the track listing without even asking you what tracks you want and in what order.

Unlike everybody else, it seems, I still look at it as an LP with a beginning and an end. But in a way we've gone back to the mid 60s, where you had one hit single and eleven duff tracks – that's how the industry wants it.

Everybody wanted 'Blindness' as track one. They're regressing, with their iPod minds. Suddenly, everybody's a connoisseur.

They did the same with Orson Welles. The studio-heads couldn't just leave his work as he intended – it was all, 'Well, what about this, Orson?' and 'I don't think this works.' What did they know?

I don't know a great deal about him. But I like the way he looked at things – especially *Citizen Kane*; how to tell a story from different angles. And his *Macbeth* – that's one of the best films I've ever seen. And *Touch of Evil* – that's great too.

An engineer gave me a tape of these commercials that Orson did in the 60s and 70s; and it had all the outtakes on it as well for these fishfinger and processed-pea commercials. It's hilarious.

He was obviously having a few money problems at the time. From *Citizen Kane* to Mrs Pickford's processed peas – it's a bit of a departure. But the funniest part of it is that he can't read the script. It doesn't add up for him. He needs to know the thread of the story. And he keeps asking questions like, 'Who wrote this?' and 'How do the fish get into the fingers?' – he's obviously drunk and he can't grasp the fundamentals behind it.

I like the way he saw life as a story; how his narrative eye was so finely honed. He was in another zone. Telling stories on stories until in the end he himself is a story. He didn't seem afraid of living in that world; and it's childish in a way, but when you can deal with it and use it, the results are evident. I think it's like heightened awareness, similar to when you don't eat for a few days or you've been on a bit of a bender – you see things differently. And not always in an obvious way.

Voices 4

How strange and sad the familiar can be. How complicated and pointless . . . I refuse to lose it in the eye of
poverty and too much beer and hearing the same voices
in the same places . . . A life lived forward can only be
understood backwards . . . And so backwards I look back
with a scalpel eye on afternoons wandering the city with
a flapping bag of cans for company; the rusted humour
of besuited men/women laughing in my face; unshaven
loners shuffling like pence . . . Sat on a park bench under
an egg-carton-grey sky; the day ahead much like those
before and seemingly after . . . And this stubborn cough
that erupts like an urban volcano . . . There used to be a
time when that was it. But it changes; your head and all
else . . . An endless pattern . . . And then the sticky
situations that once disabled the days return as experience, hard fought . . . and this then is a new life, a new
tale . . . And onwards.

Outro
The White Angel

And to end . . .

Do not worry – The White Angel will re-form in your midst
in the near future, my friends.

All the best,

Yr pal.

M.E.S.

Acknowledgements

Austin Collings would like to thank the following people who were there when it mattered while this book was being written. First and foremost, Mum and Dad (Joan and Michael), whose advice, born from the Golden Age of plain common sense and thoughtful stoicism, is always appreciated. And, more importantly, thanks for letting me have so many days off school to dream and fall into music, burn through books, devour films and think of myself as different. It was the best education a boy could ever have had.

And the rest of the family – Mark, Jonathan, Beverley and the two most gorgeous girls on this blue and green ball: Hope and Milly.

And in no particular order, for you're all as priceless as one another:

Tommy Dunn and Tommy Dunn Jr – you couldn't ask for two better diamonds; long may our adventures continue – James Ricks, Phil Hayes, Nicola Probert, George Shaw, Chris Ogden, Dodge, Joanne O'Connor, James Fennings, Jimmy Muffin, The Neck, The Dudes, Estelle, Amy Lee, and all those in America who helped show me what a truly wondrous place it is, Michael Bracewell, Mark Hodkinson, Ian Travis and the Guidance Centre, Mark Alcroft, Ian Littlewood, Graham and Andrew Madeley, Sorry John, Emmanuel Ohajah, Mark Chambers, Ian Walker, Richard and Danny Murphy, Oliver McCombe, Joe Devlin, Mark Kennedy, Dan Davies, Michael Gildare, Steve and Laura: all of whom, at some point, have 'seen me right' when I've been low in the pocket or helped re-remind me that writing a book is preferable to sitting in a chewing-gum-grey office, bored witless, thinking of better elsewheres – cheers.

Thanks are also due to the always-patient and optimistic literary agent that is David Luxton; and to the long-suffering but good-humoured Tony Lacey, and everyone else at Penguin who had a hand in helping.

And to Mark and Elena for letting me work on something truly unforgettable and life-changing.

He just wanted a decent book to read ...

Not too much to ask, is it? It was in 1935 when Allen Lane, Managing Director of Bodley Head Publishers, stood on a platform at Exeter railway station looking for something good to read on his journey back to London. His choice was limited to popular magazines and poor-quality paperbacks – the same choice faced every day by the vast majority of readers, few of whom could afford hardbacks. Lane's disappointment and subsequent anger at the range of books generally available led him to found a company – and change the world.

'We believed in the existence in this country of a vast reading public for intelligent books at a low price, and staked everything on it'
Sir Allen Lane, 1902–1970, founder of Penguin Books

The quality paperback had arrived – and not just in bookshops. Lane was adamant that his Penguins should appear in chain stores and tobacconists, and should cost no more than a packet of cigarettes.

Reading habits (and cigarette prices) have changed since 1935, but Penguin still believes in publishing the best books for everybody to enjoy. We still believe that good design costs no more than bad design, and we still believe that quality books published passionately and responsibly make the world a better place.

So wherever you see the little bird – whether it's on a piece of prize-winning literary fiction or a celebrity autobiography, political tour de force or historical masterpiece, a serial-killer thriller, reference book, world classic or a piece of pure escapism – you can bet that it represents the very best that the genre has to offer.

Whatever you like to read – trust Penguin.